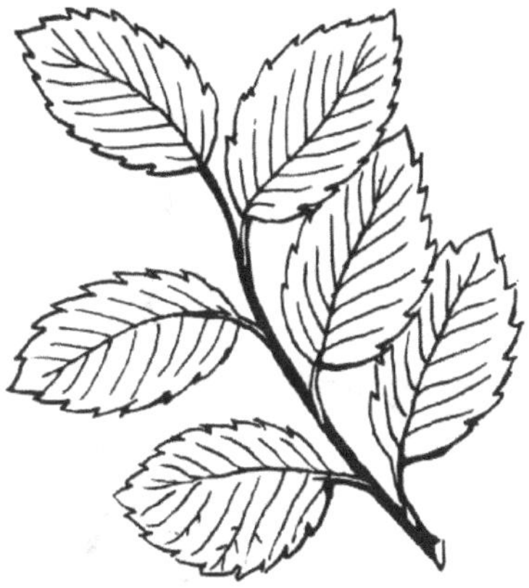

This Coloring Book Belongs To:

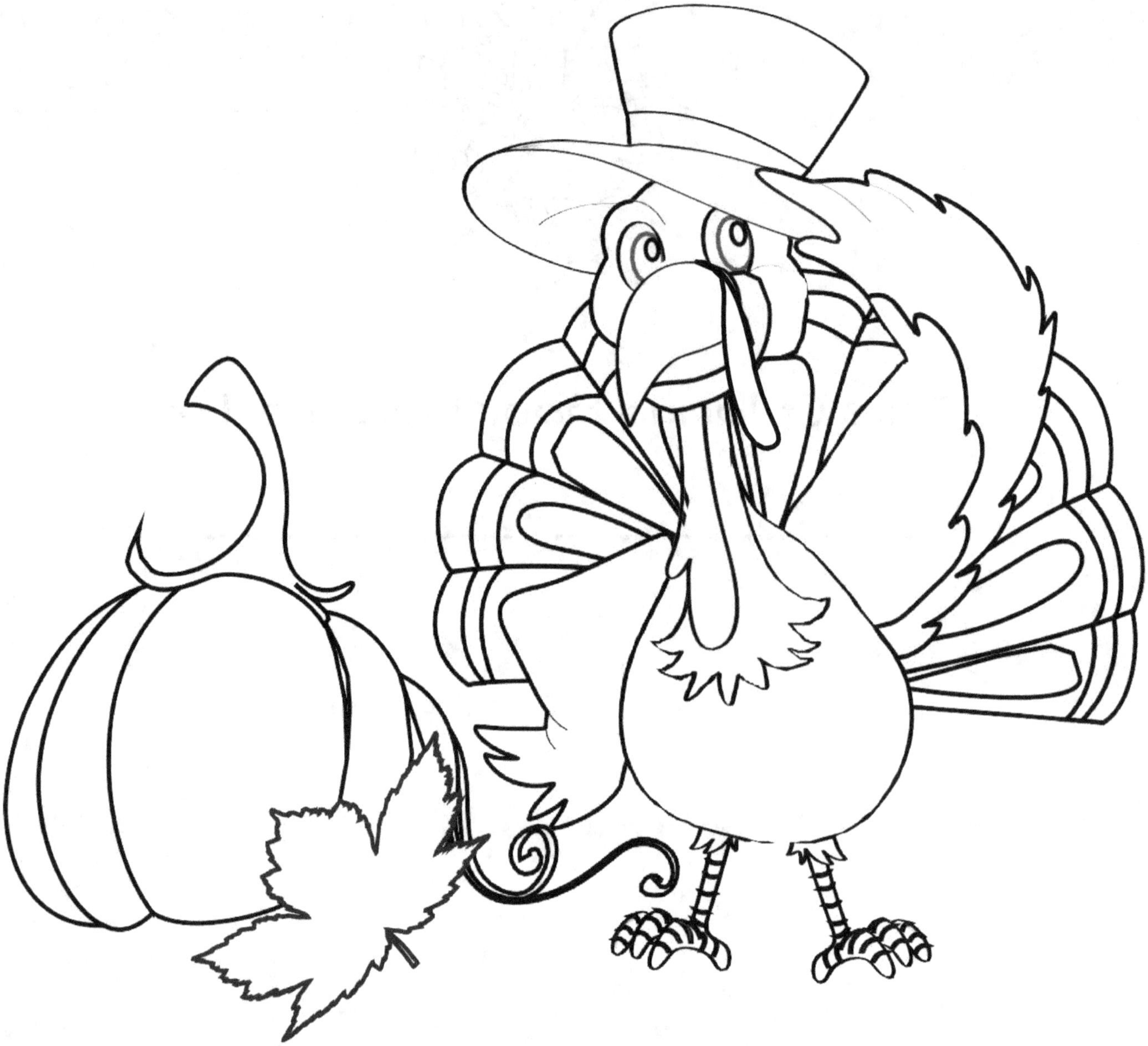

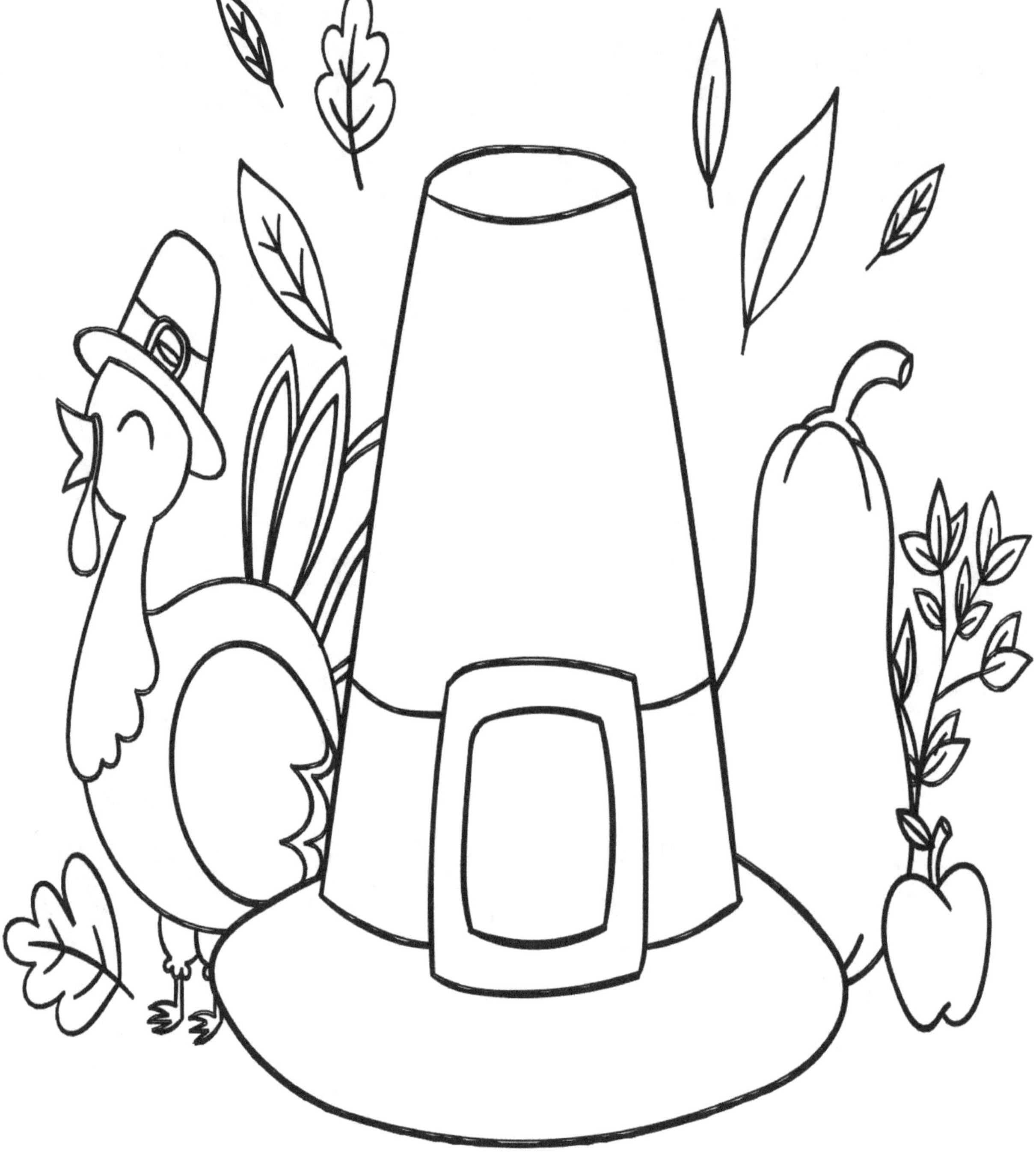

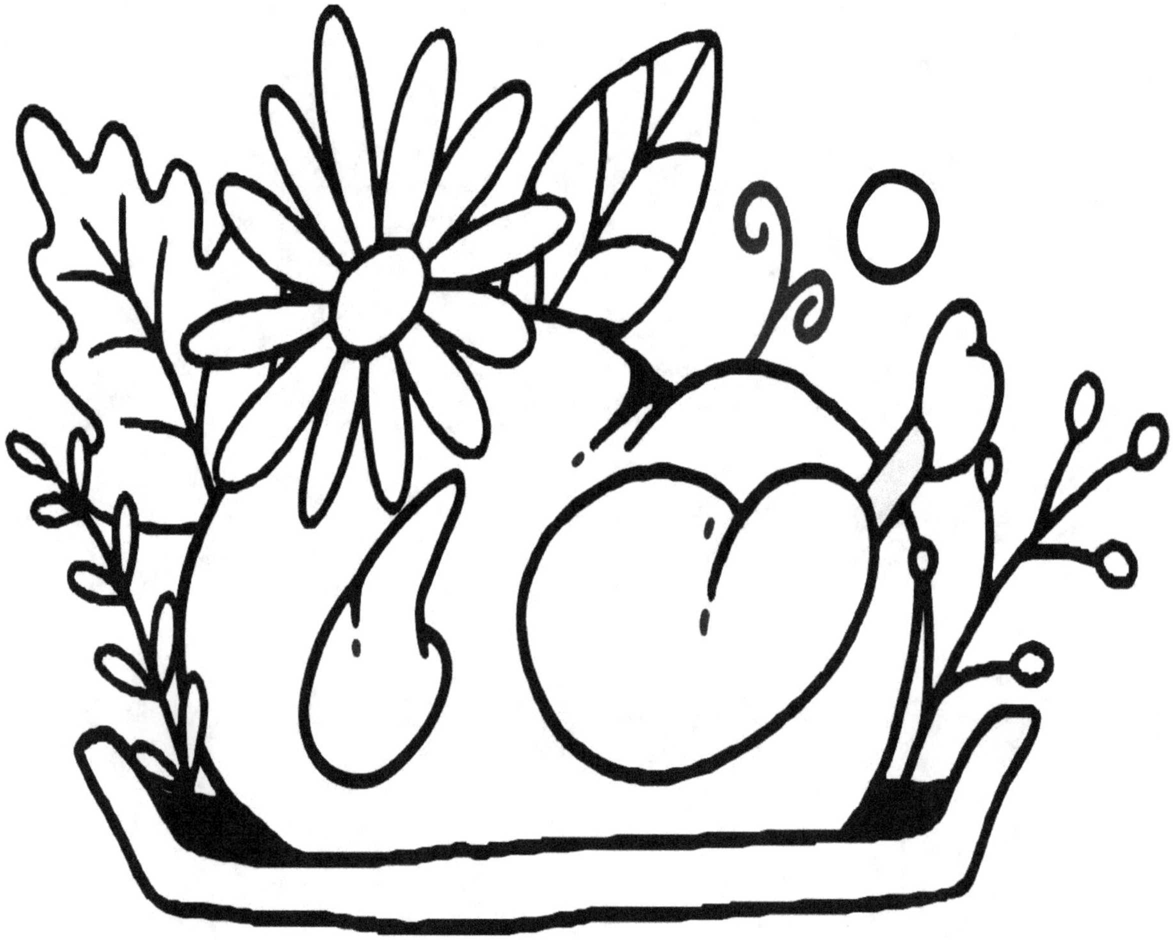

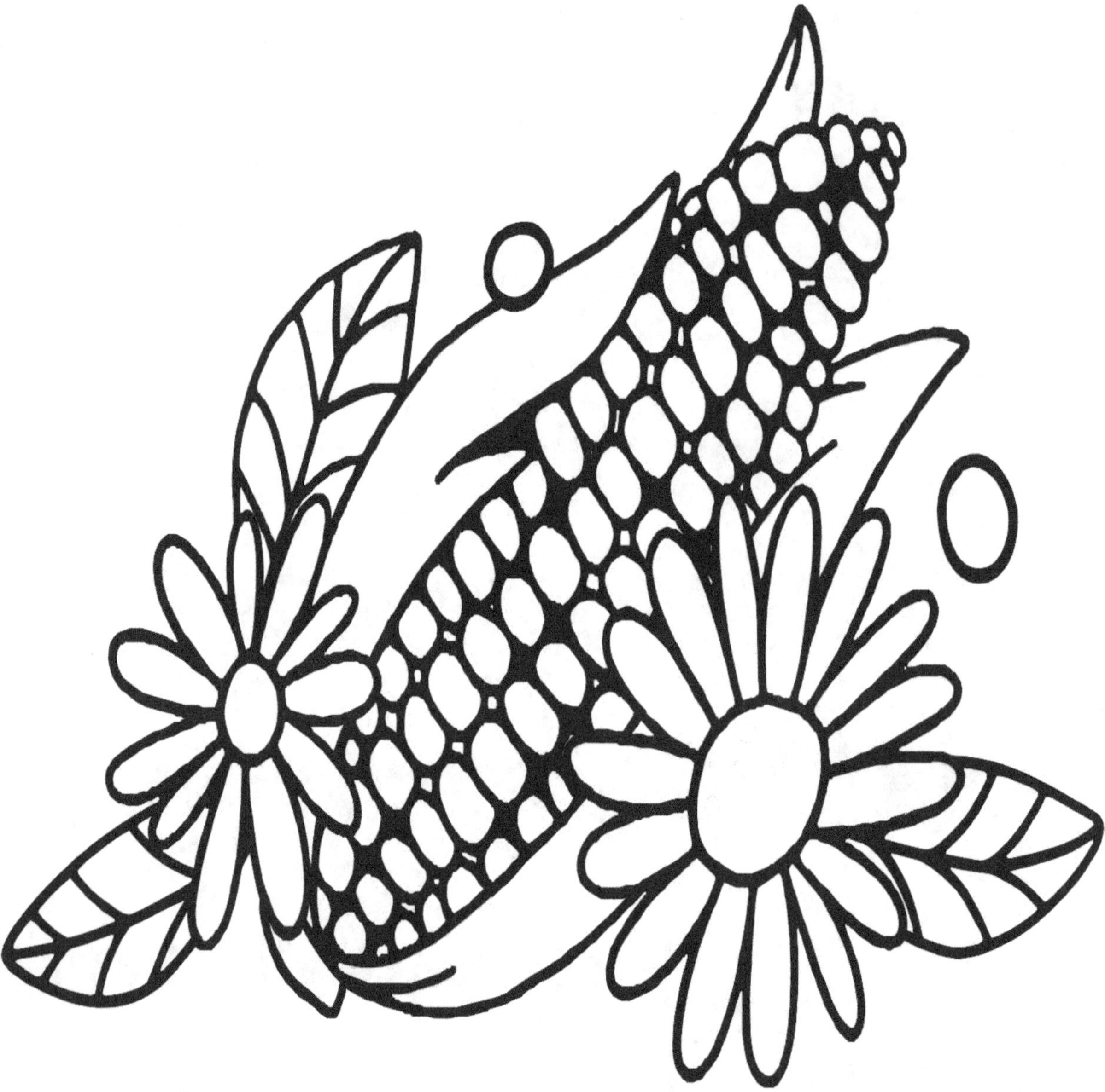

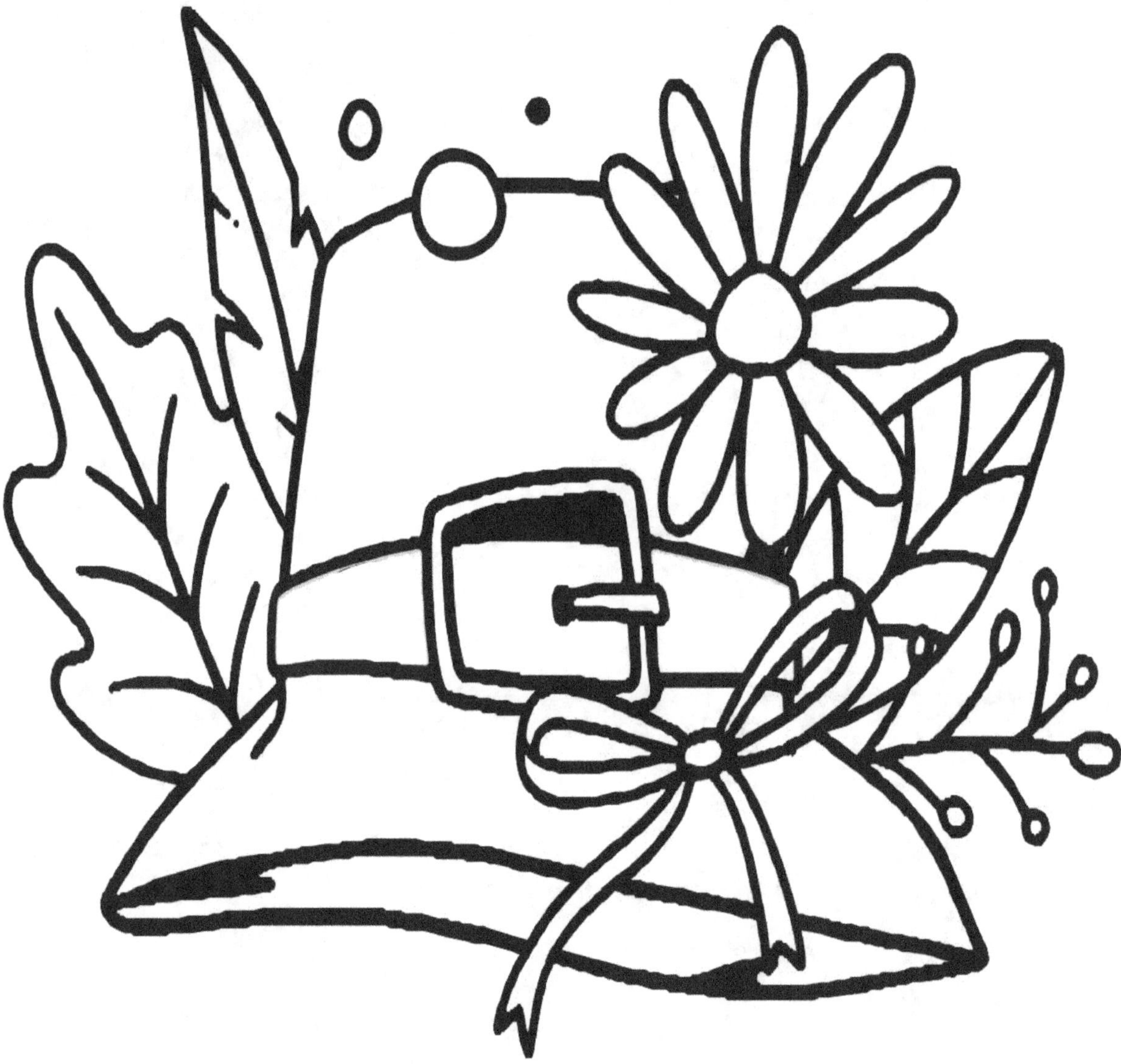

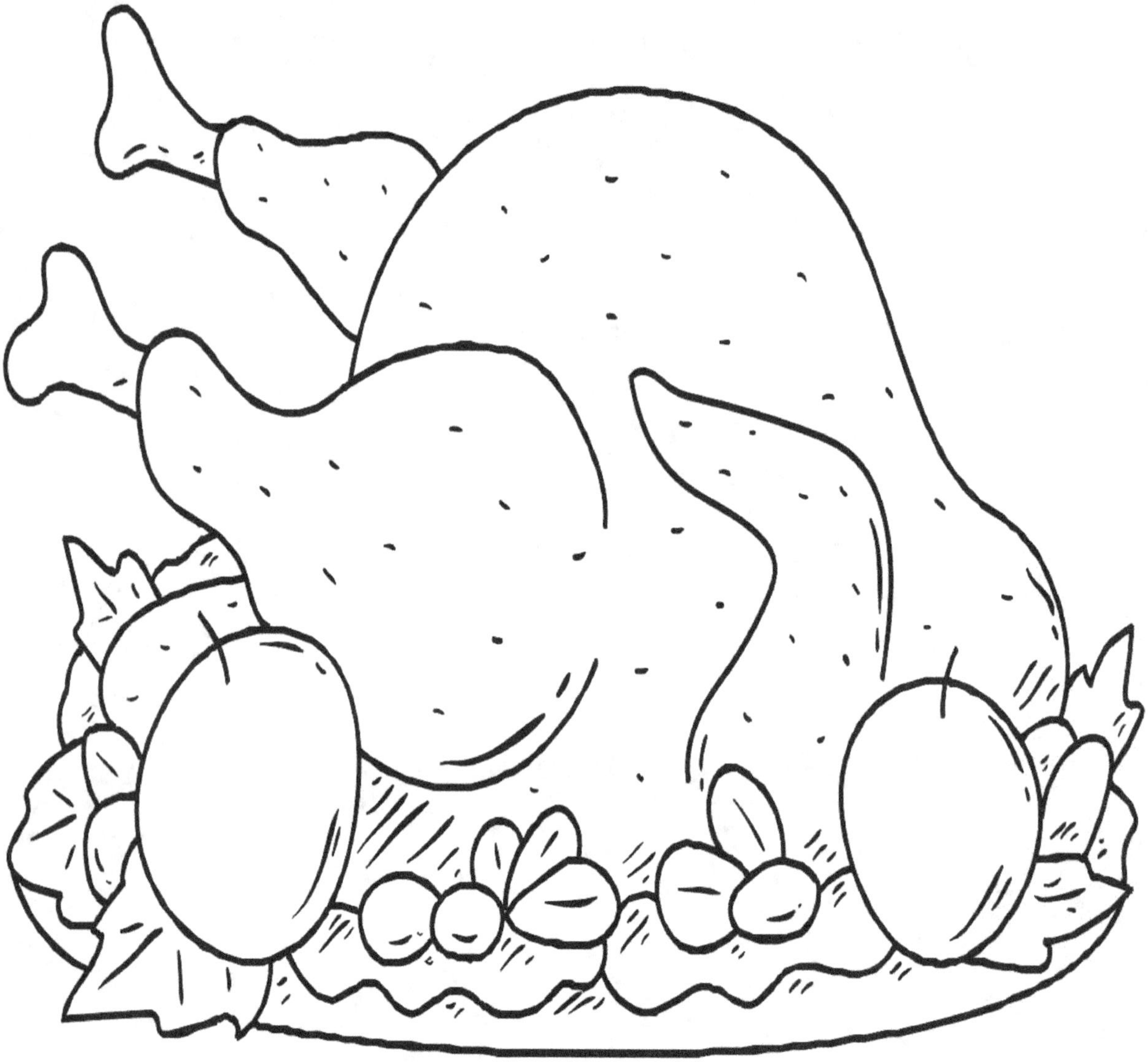

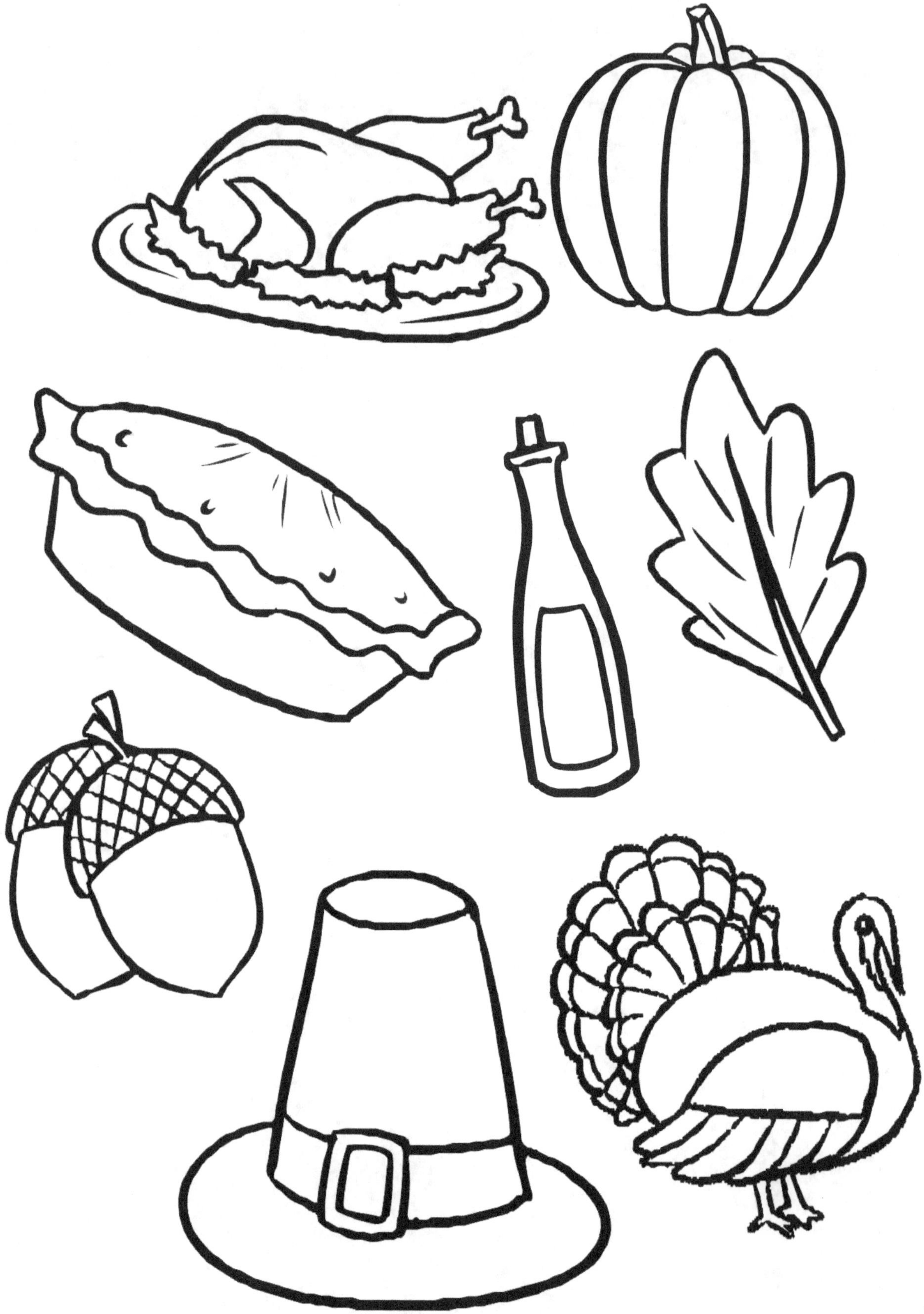

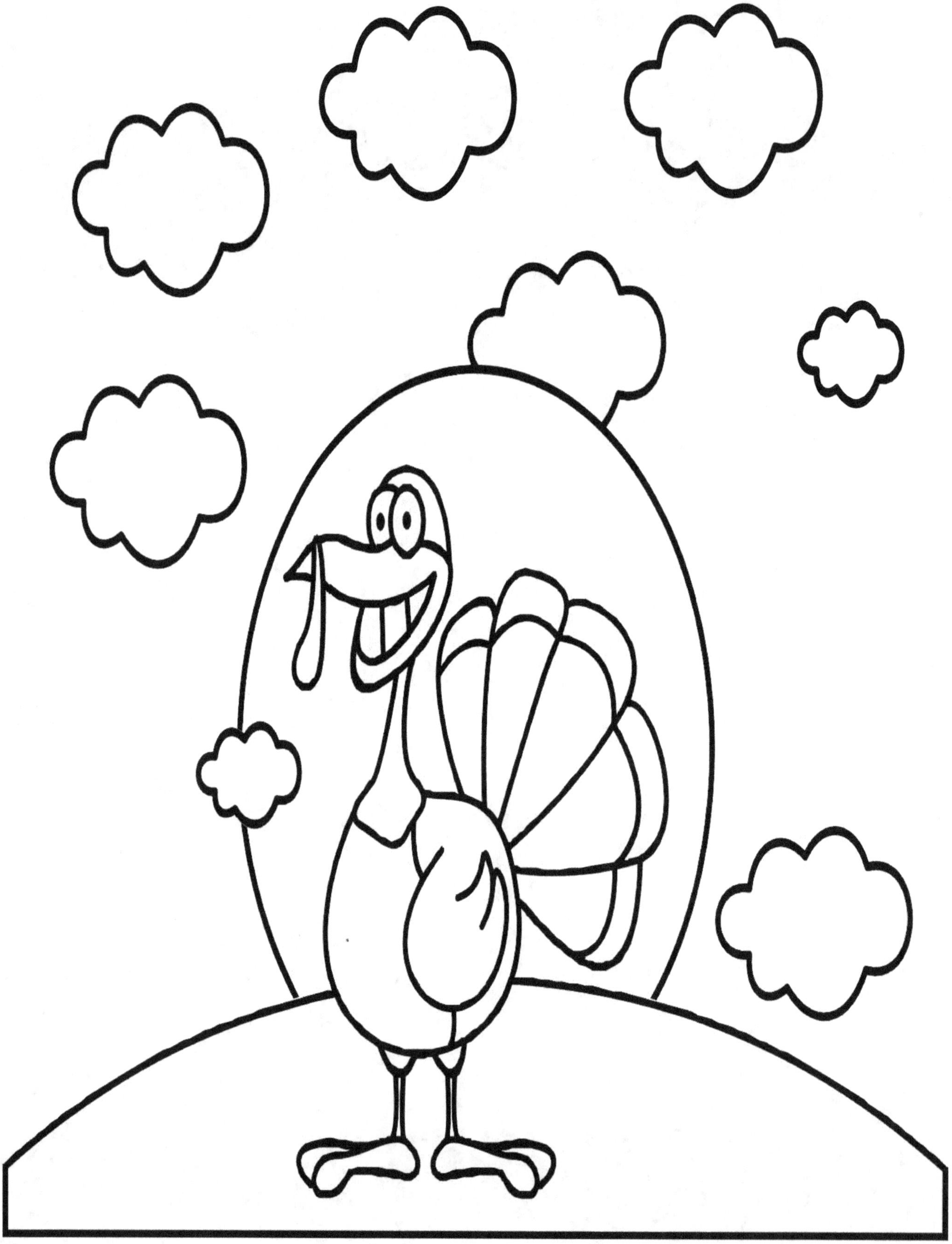

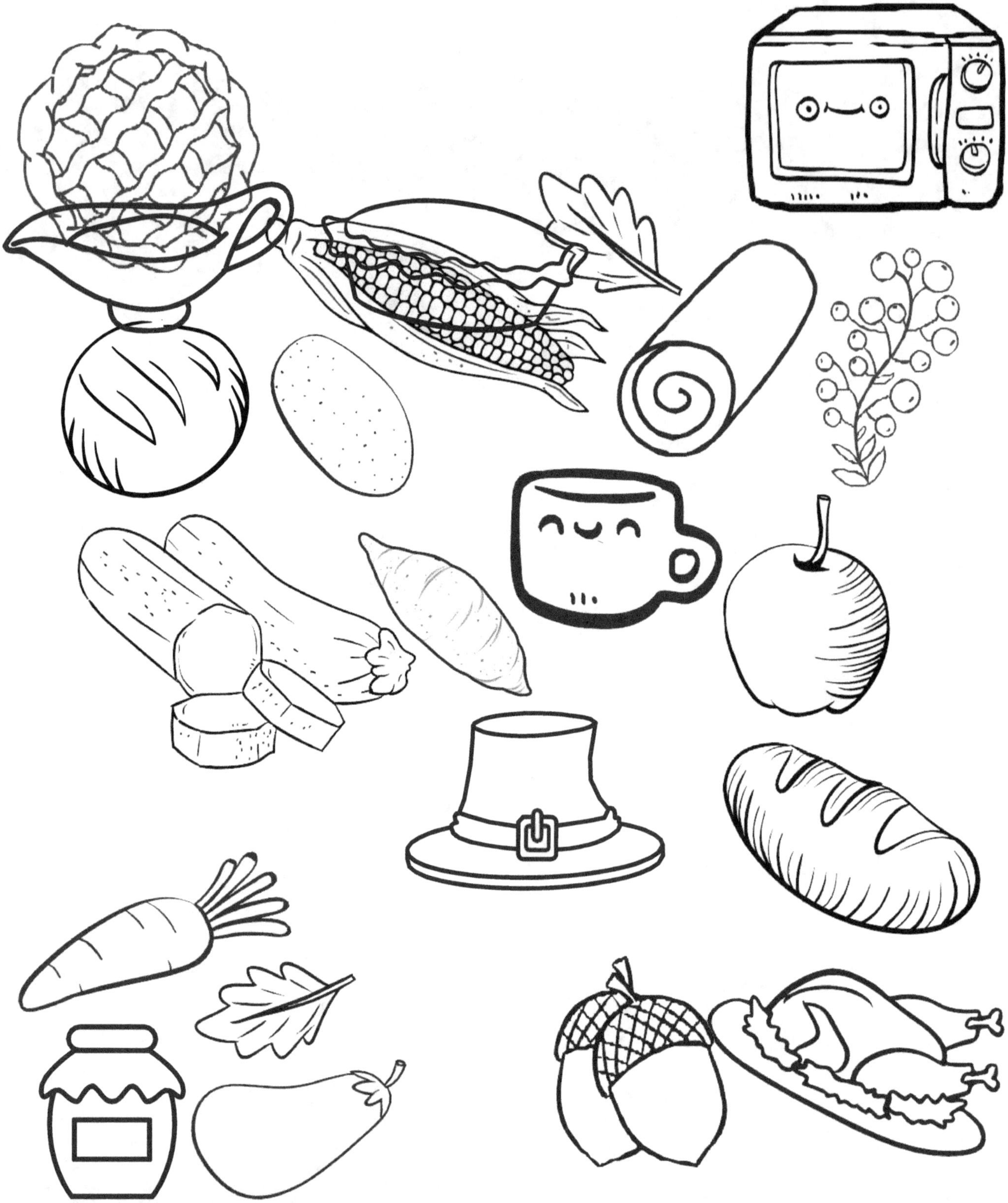

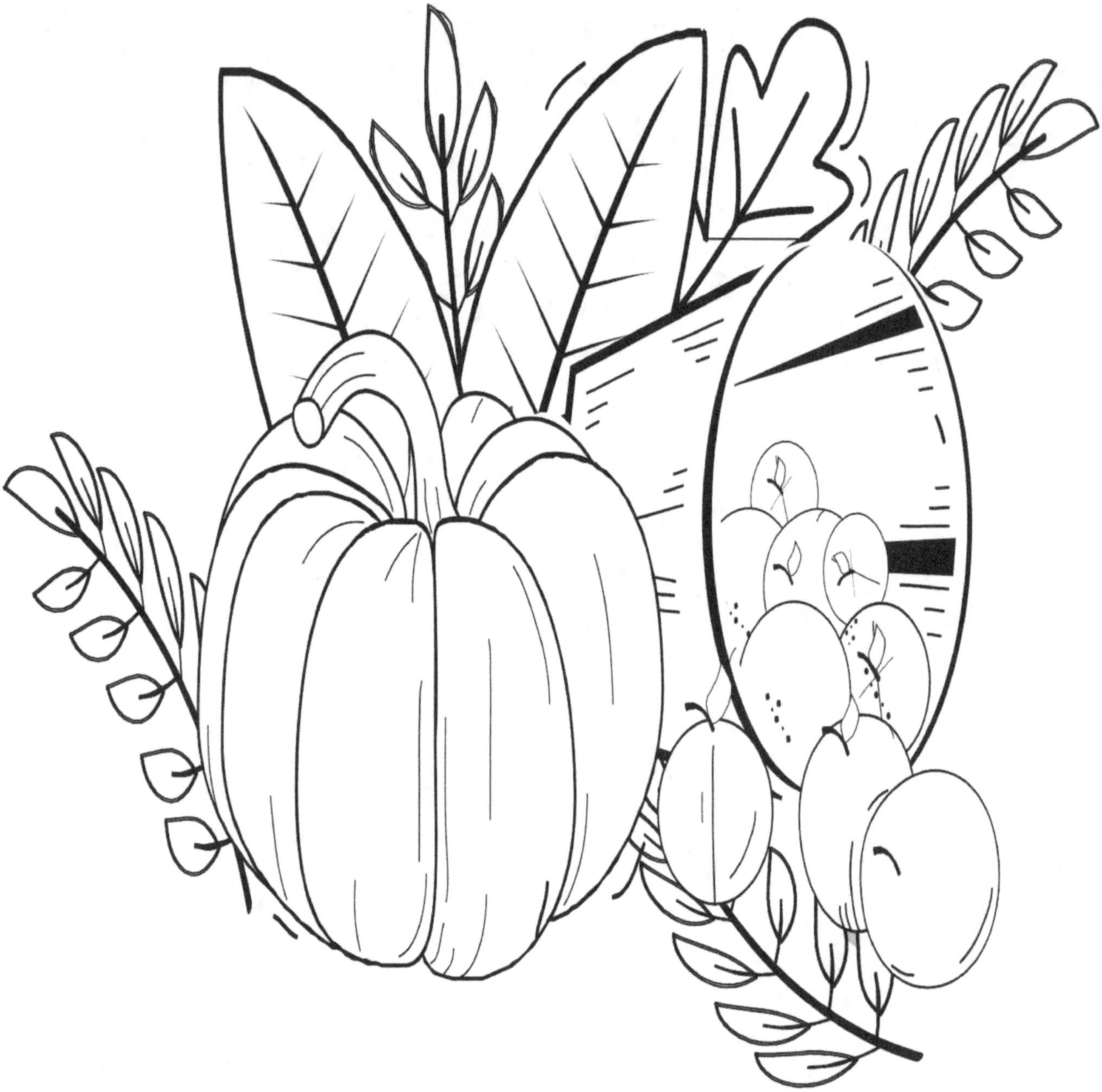

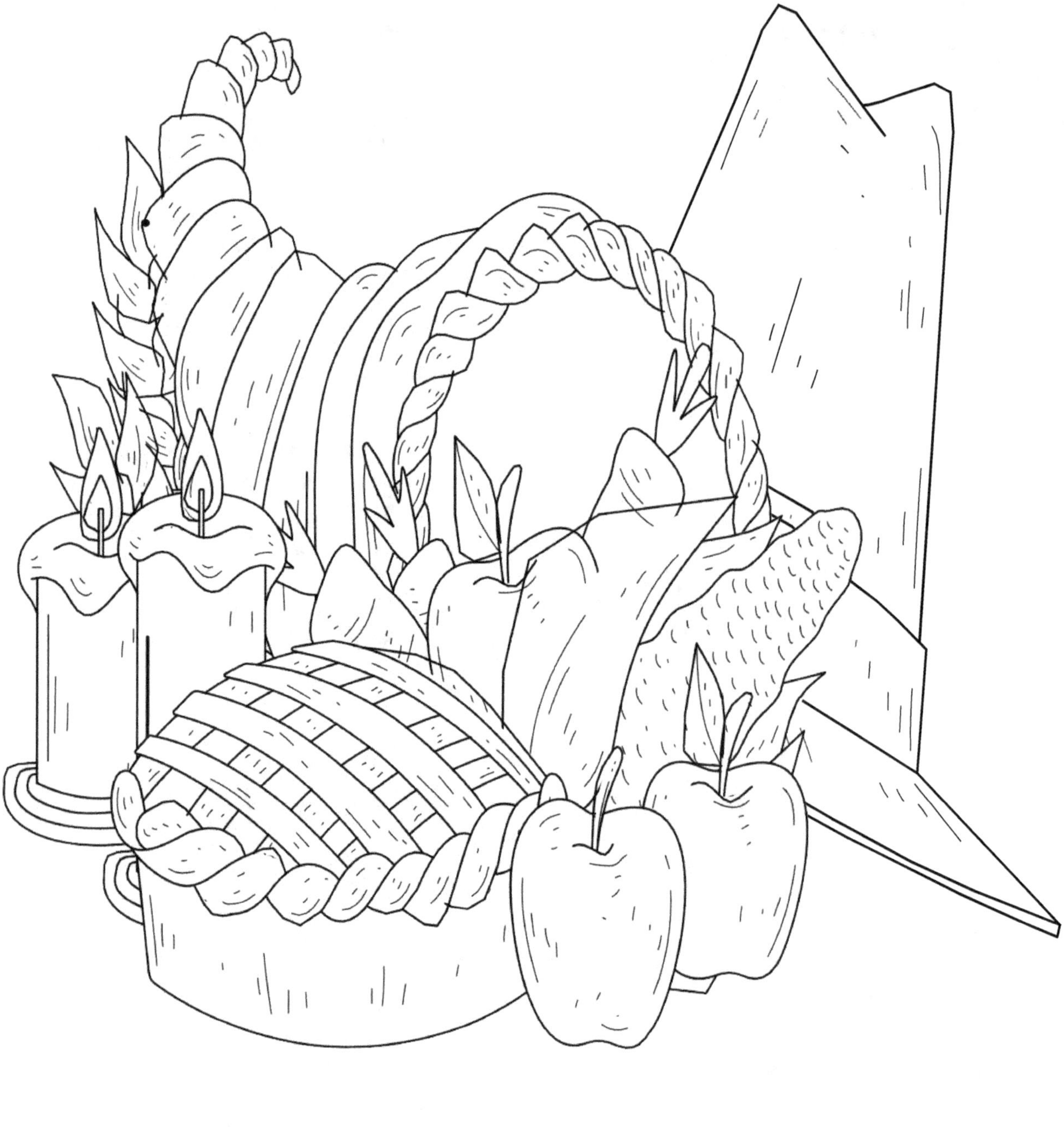

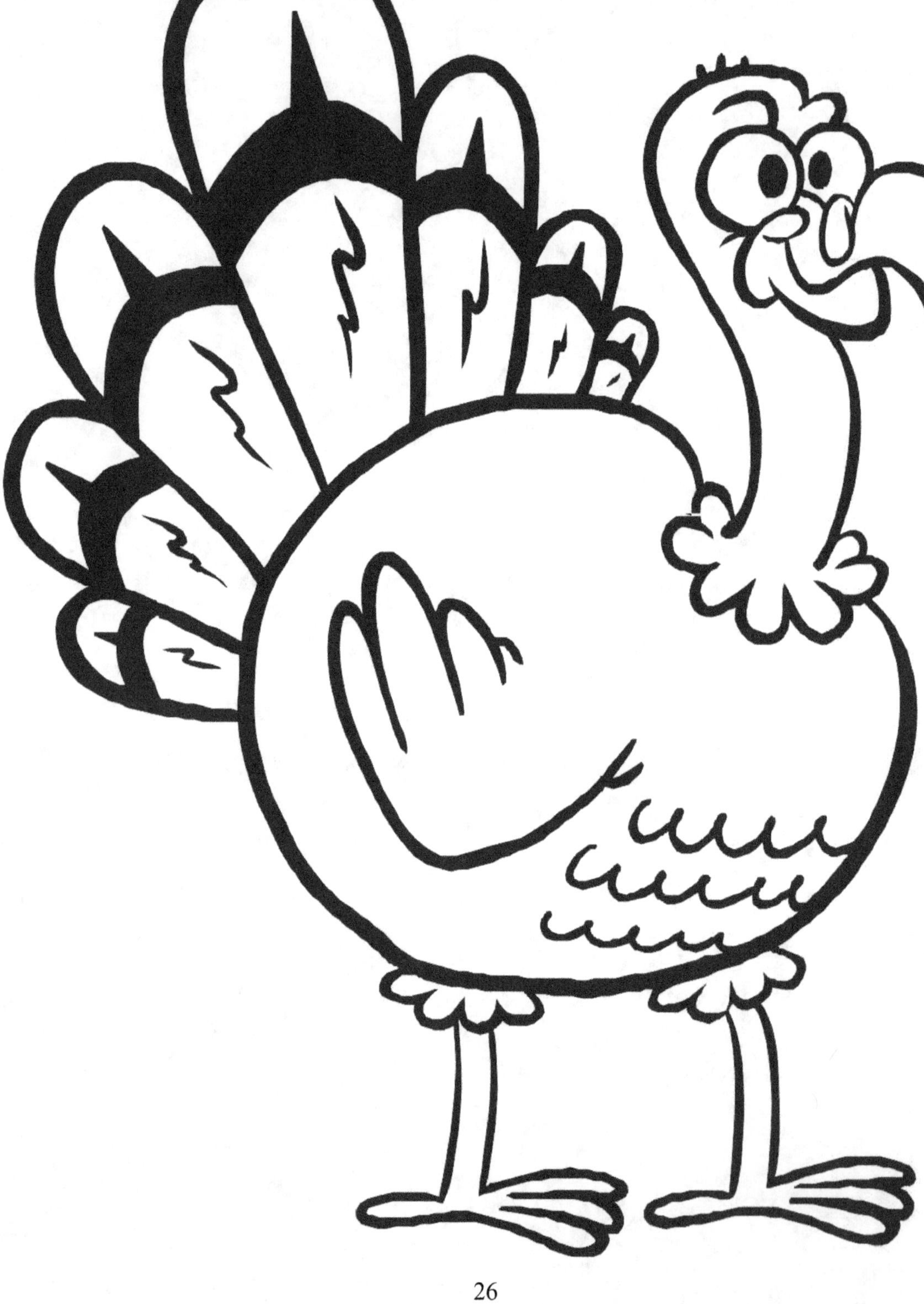

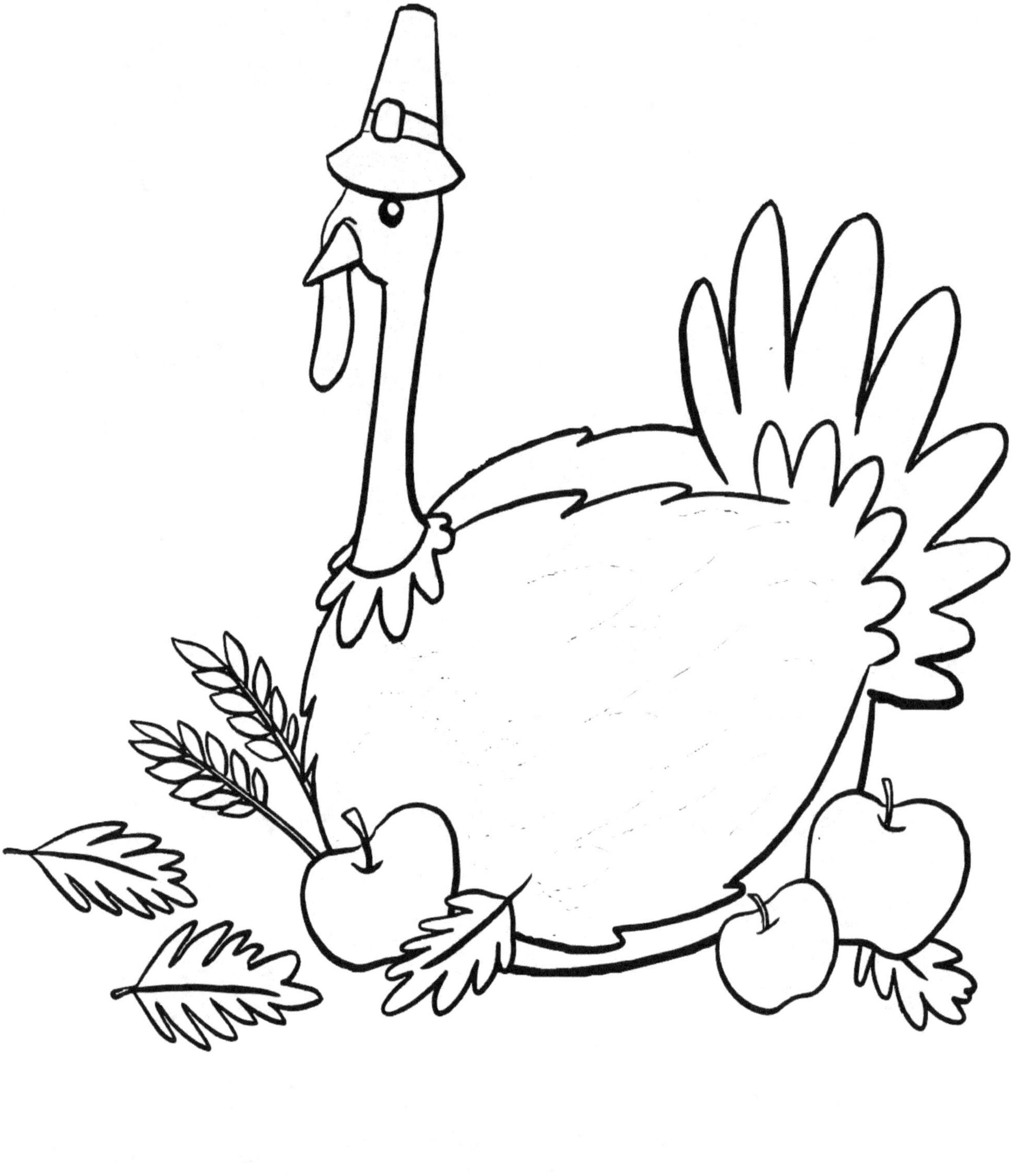

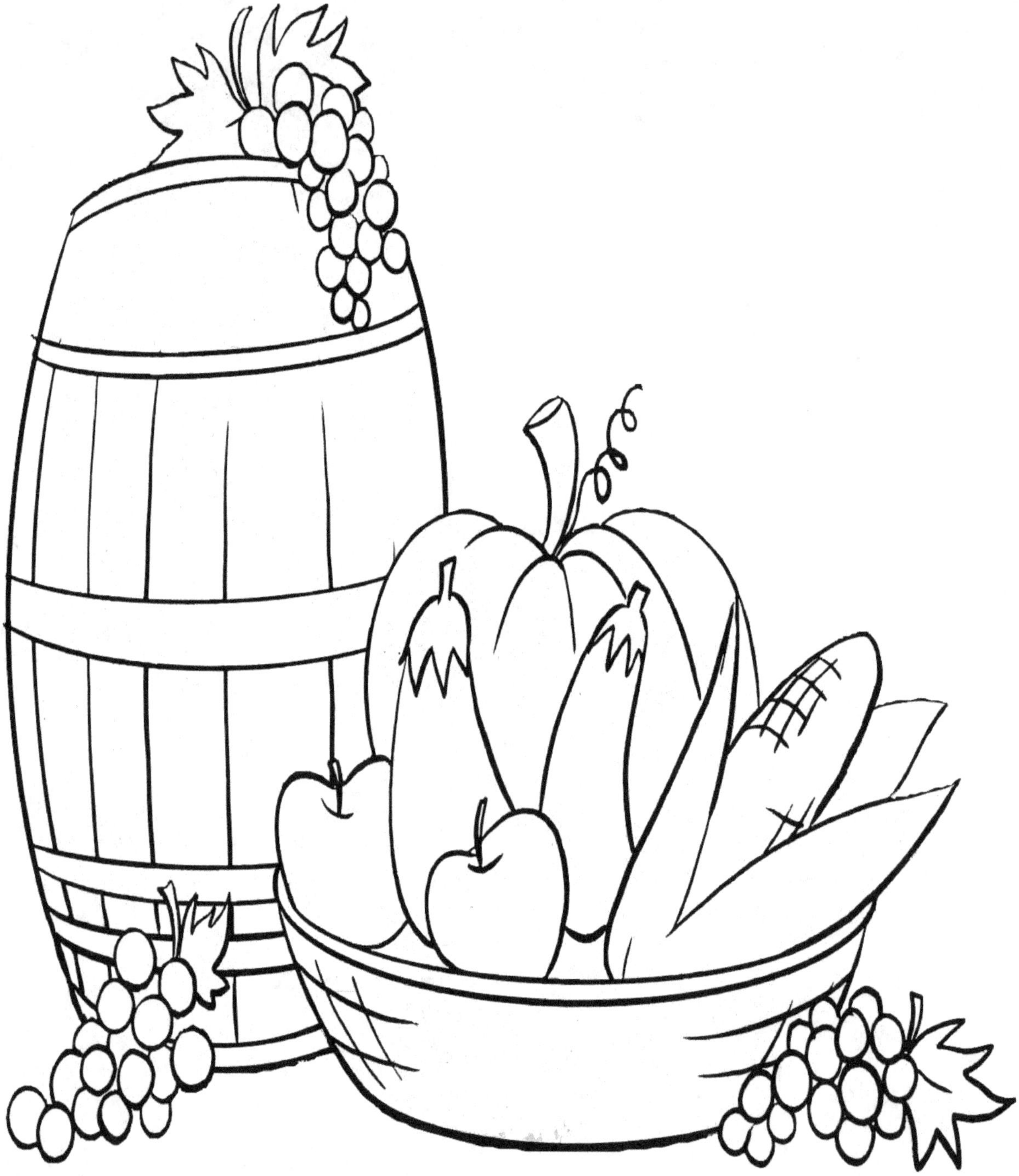

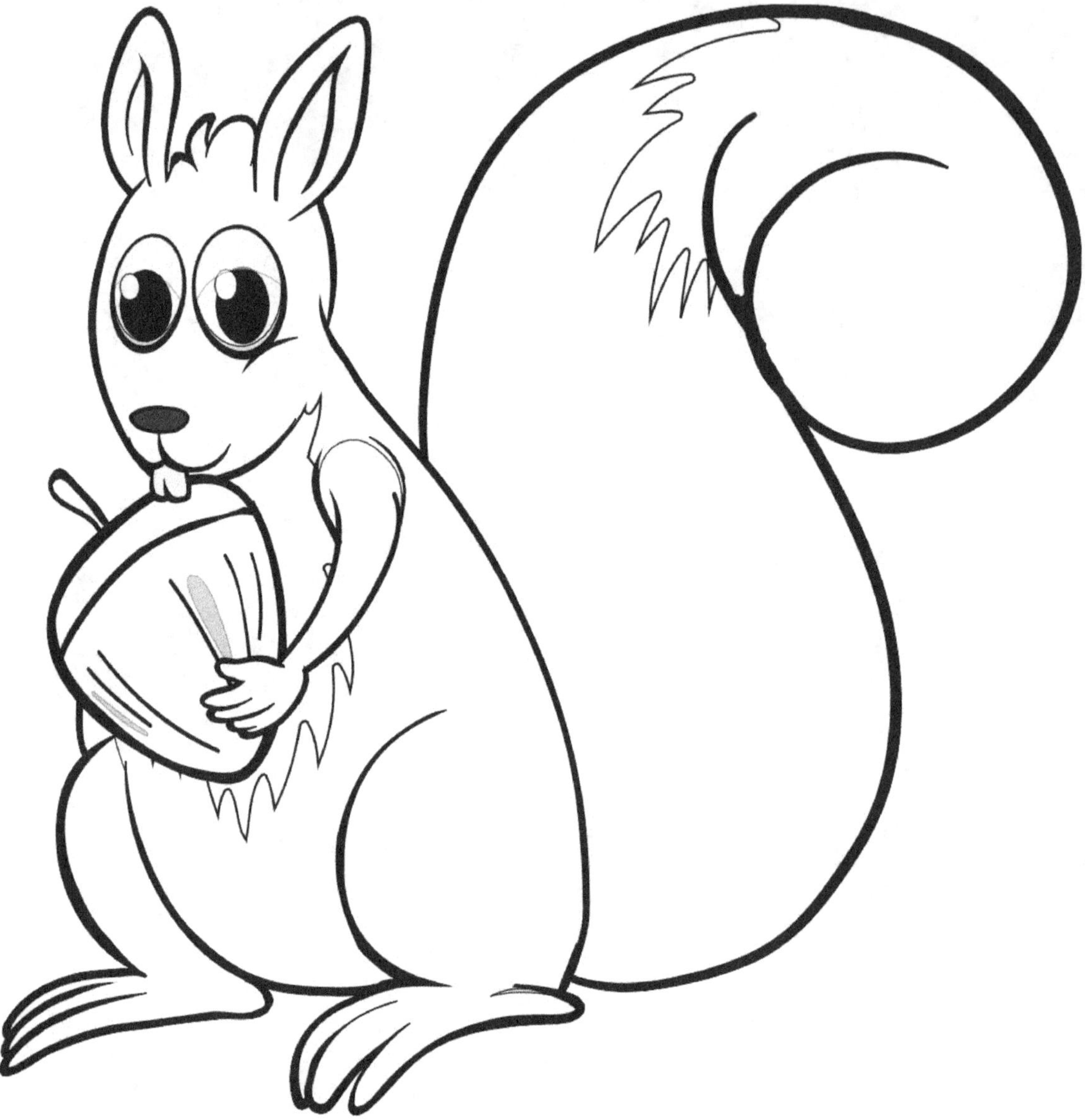

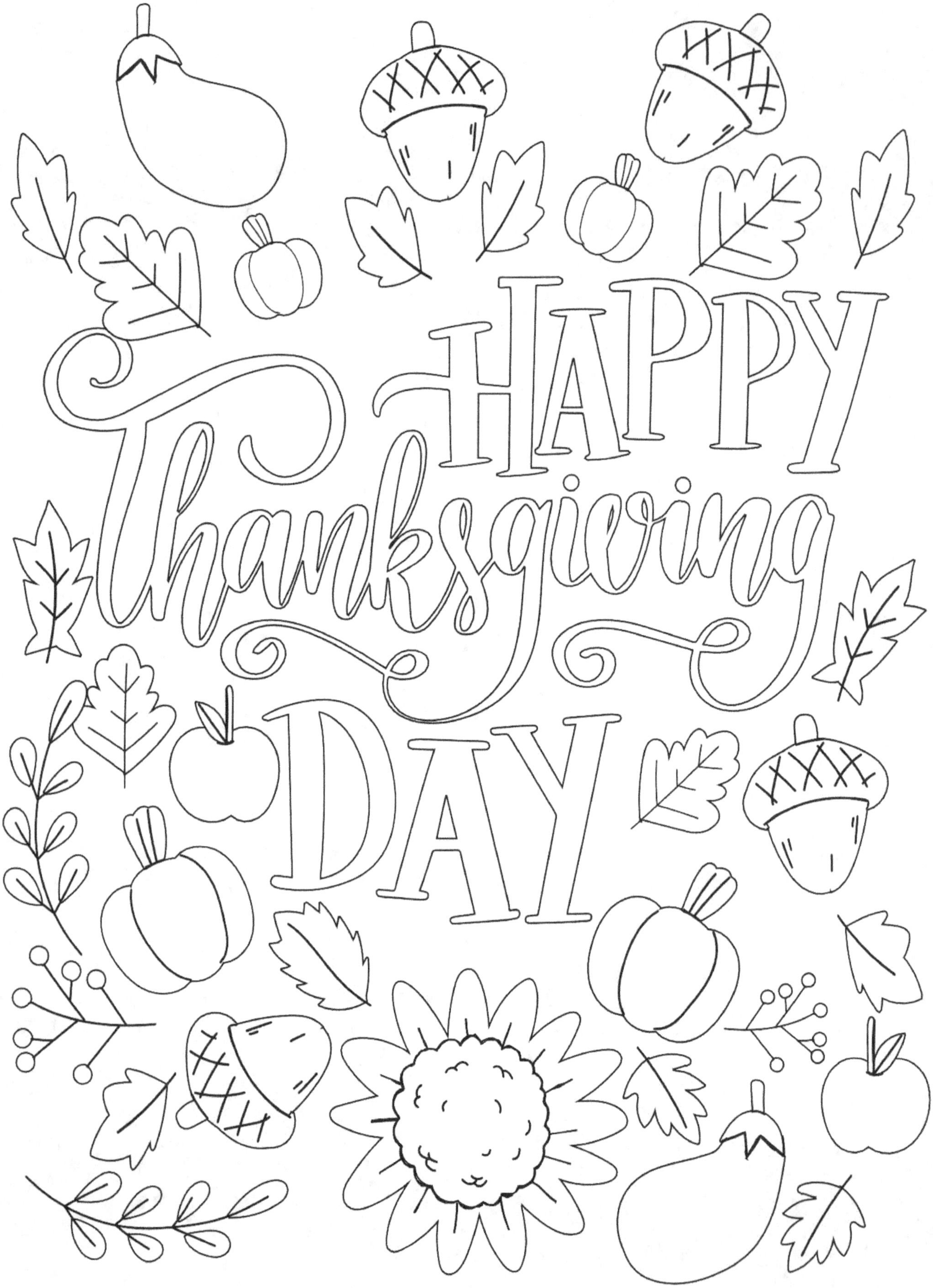
HAPPY
Thanksgiving
DAY

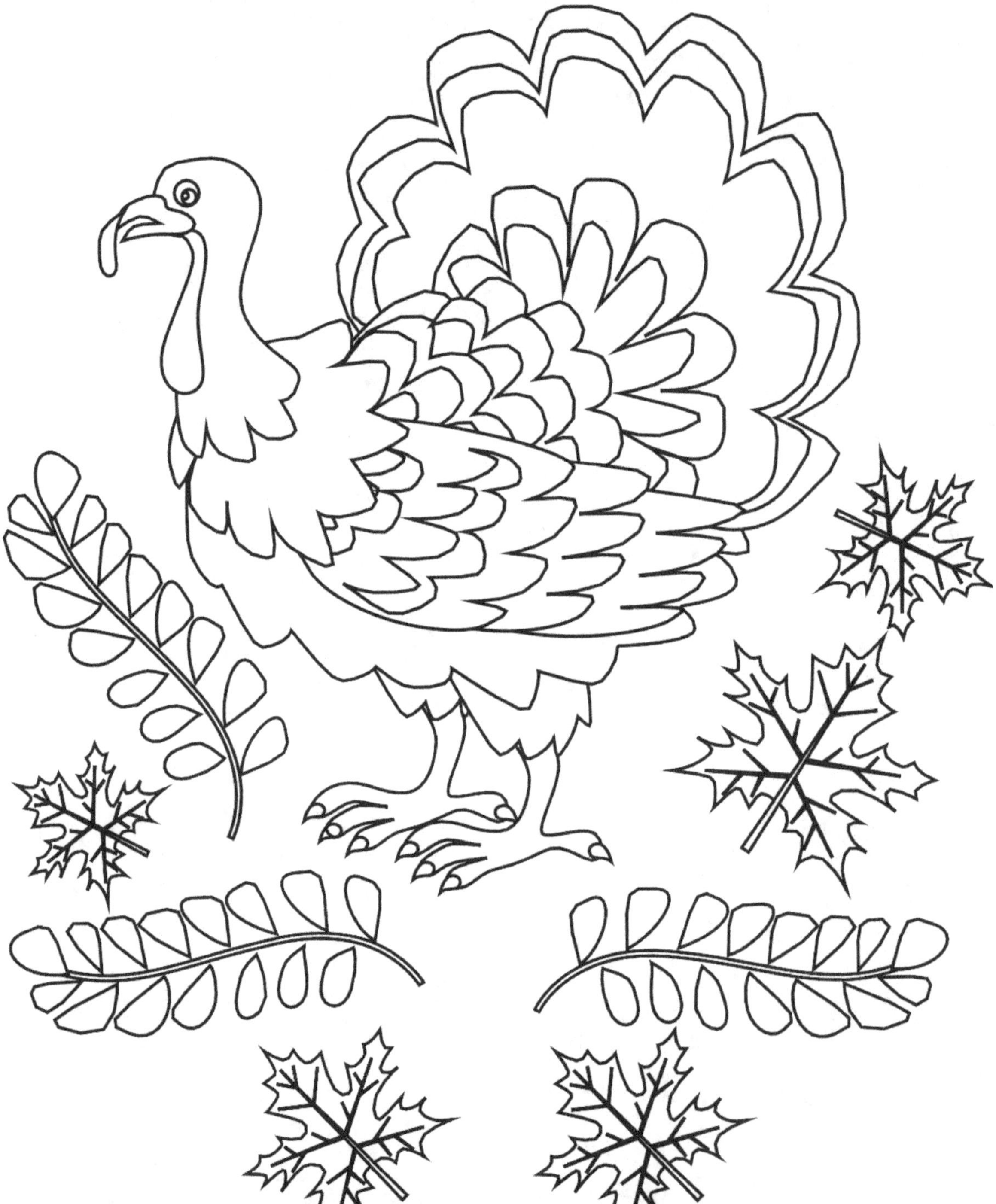

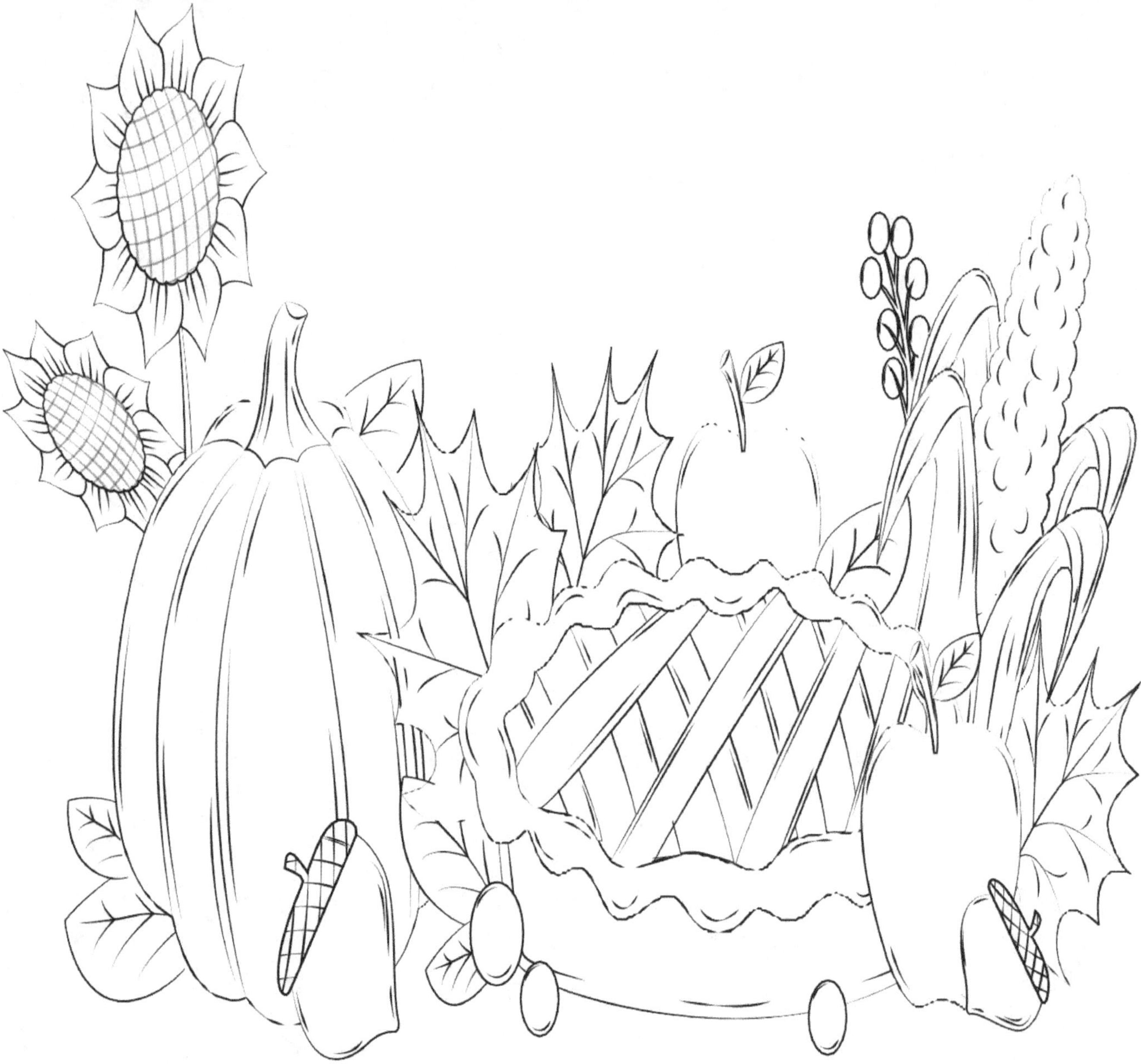

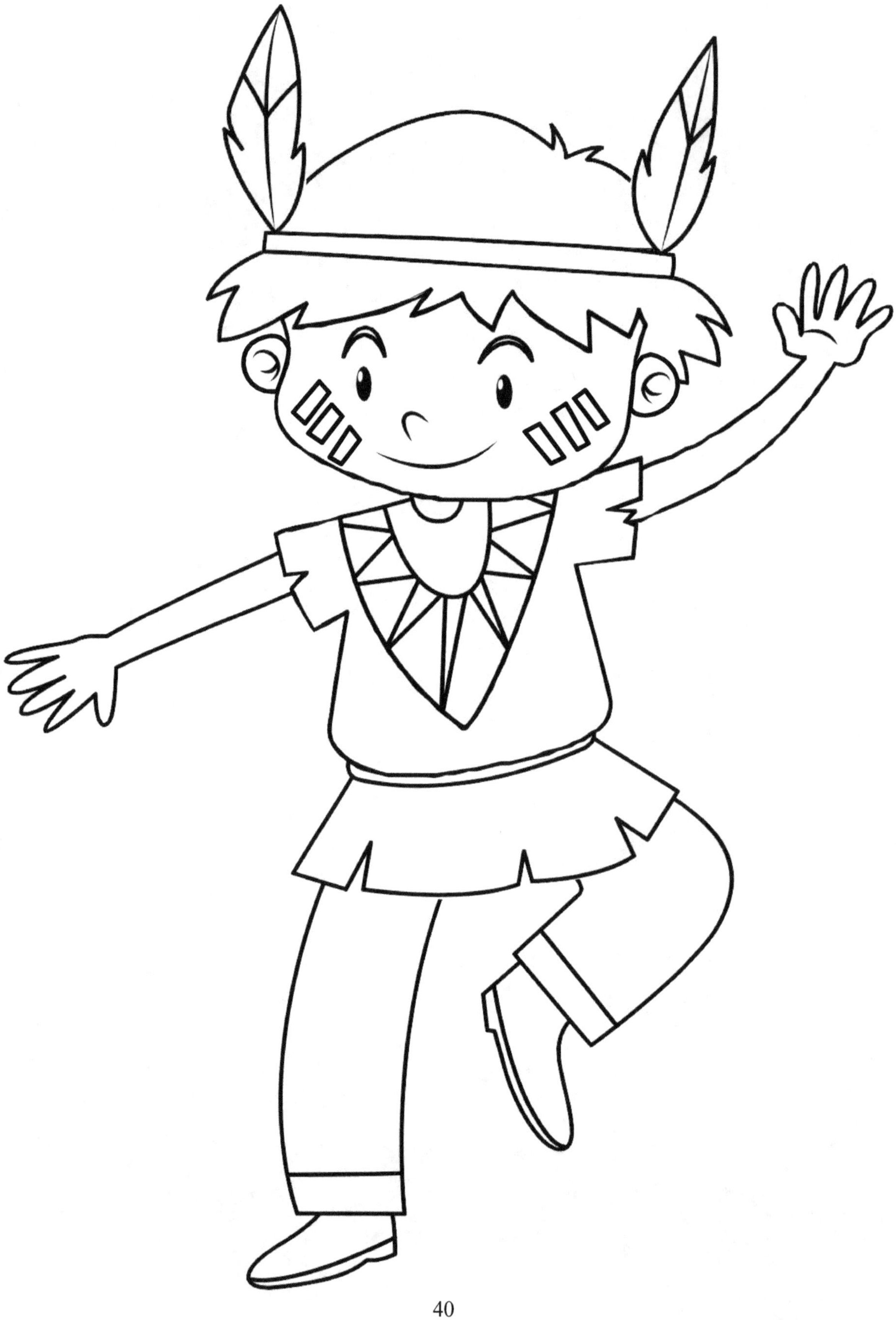

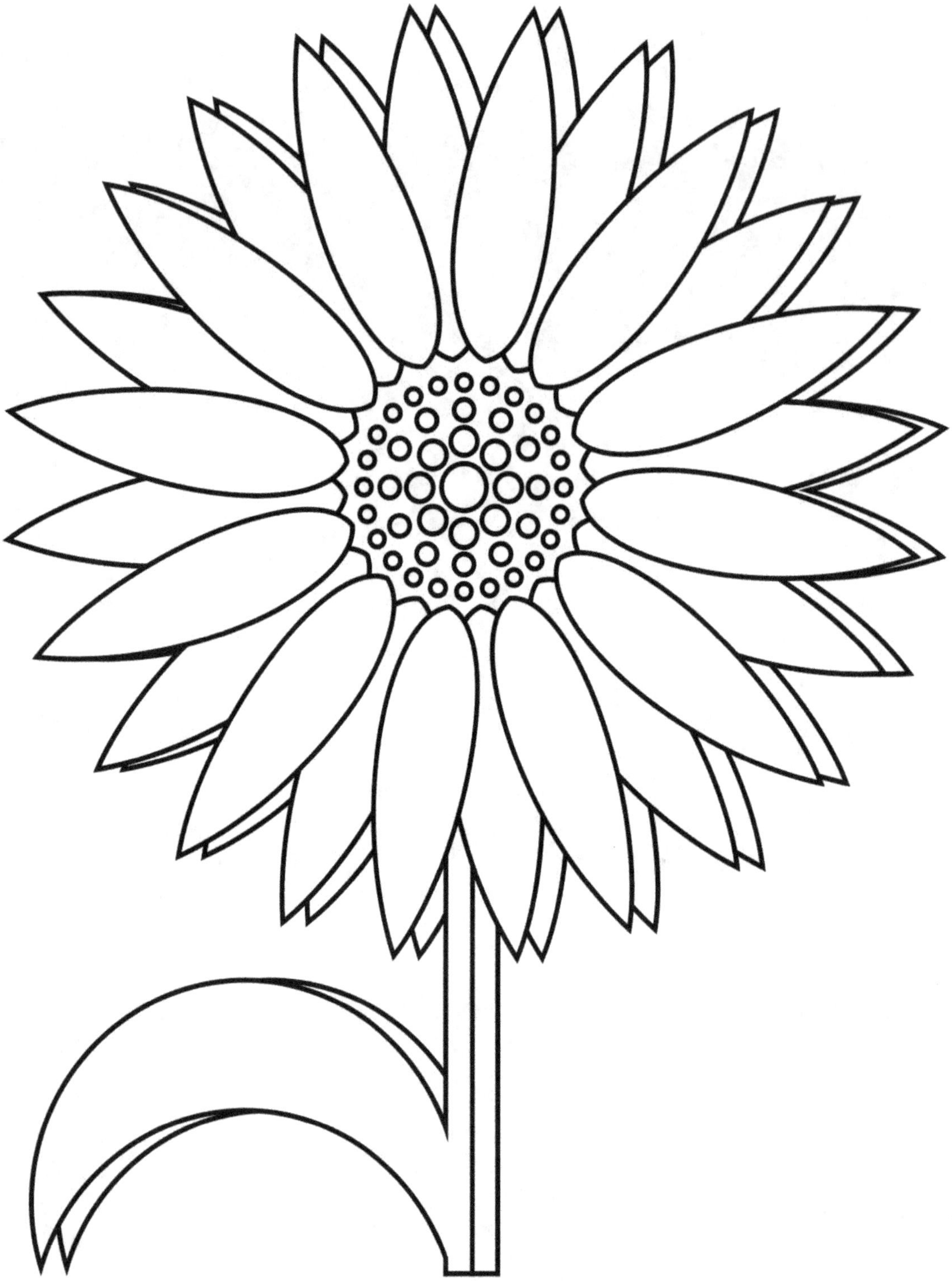

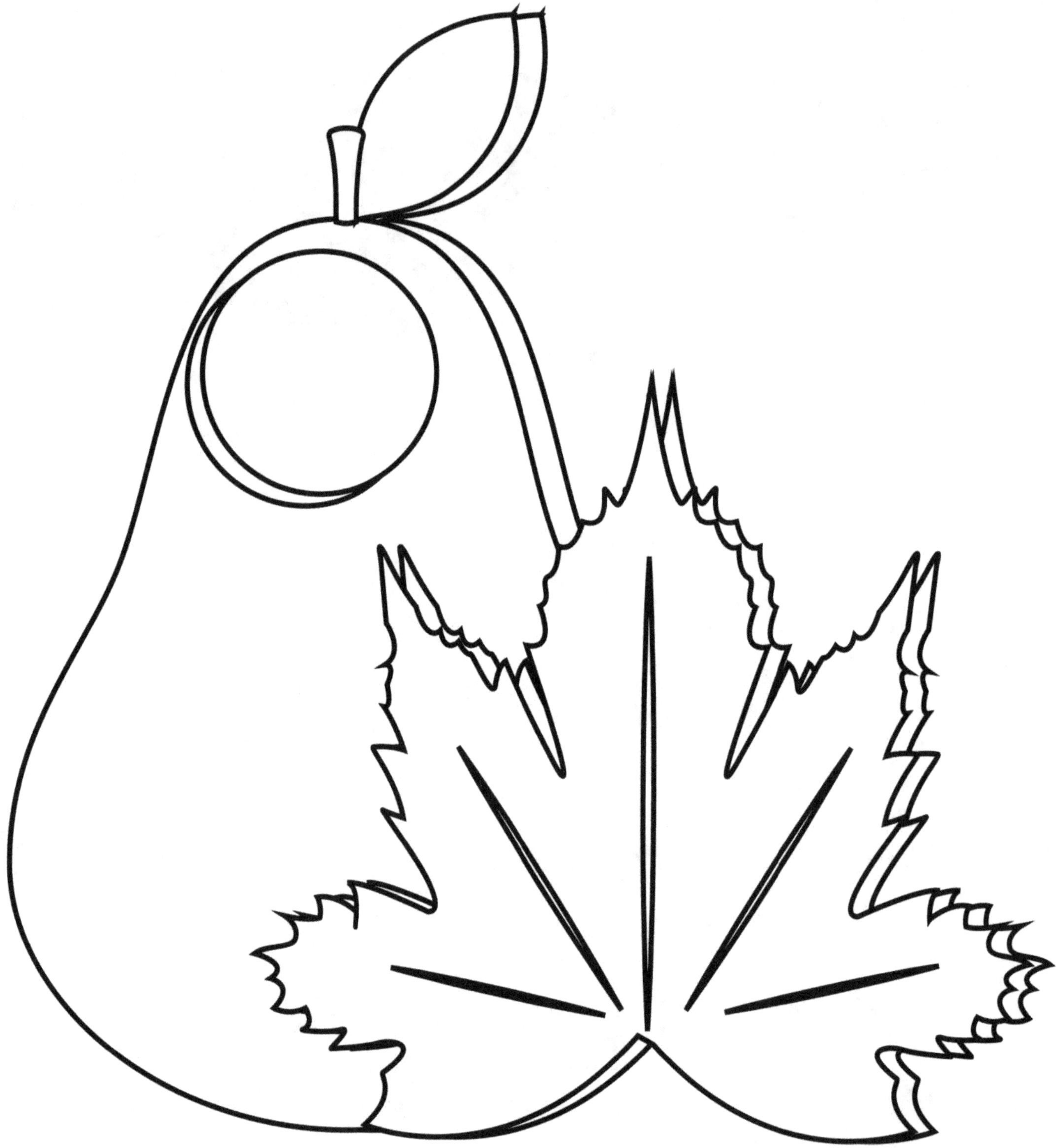

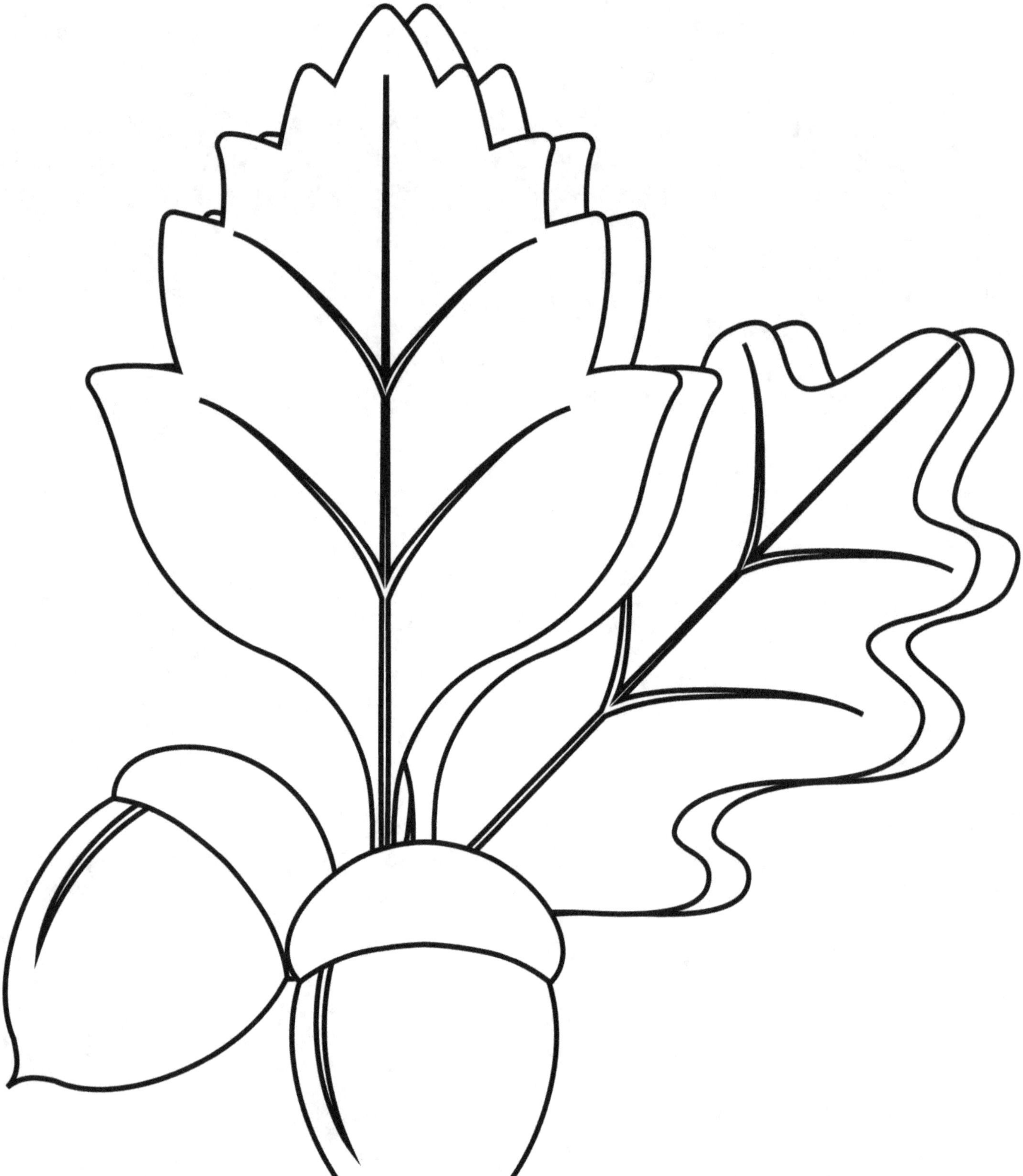

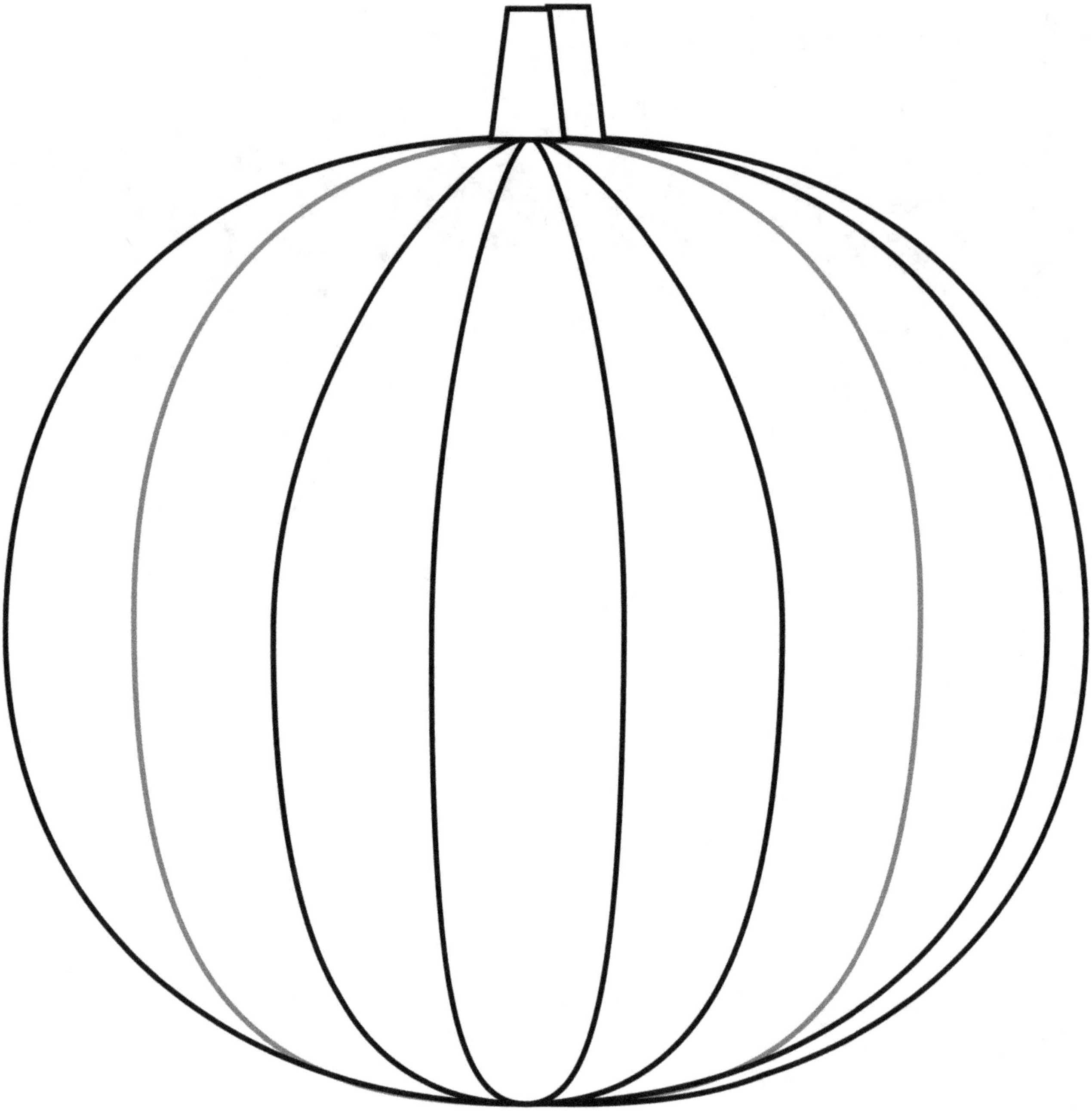

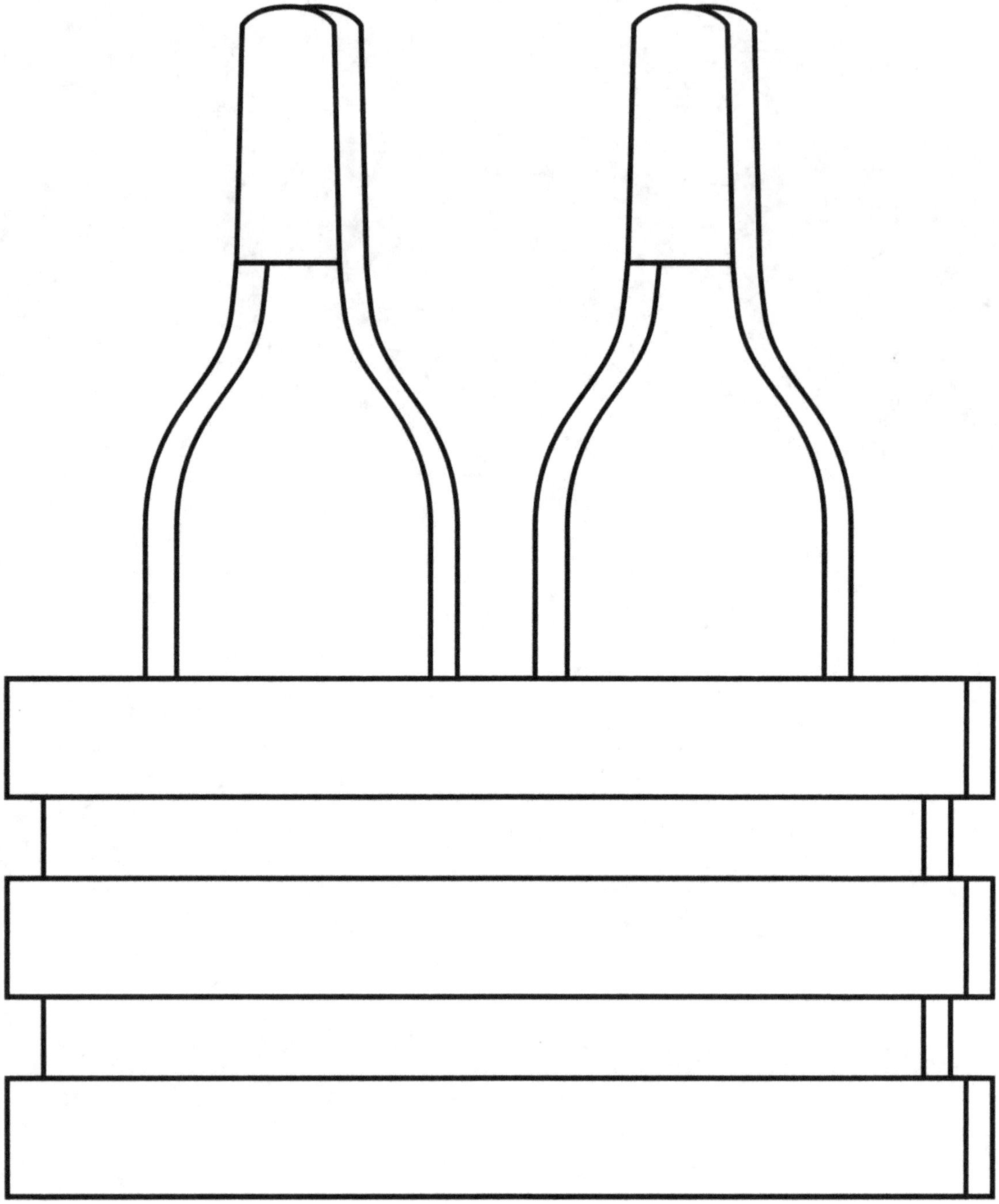

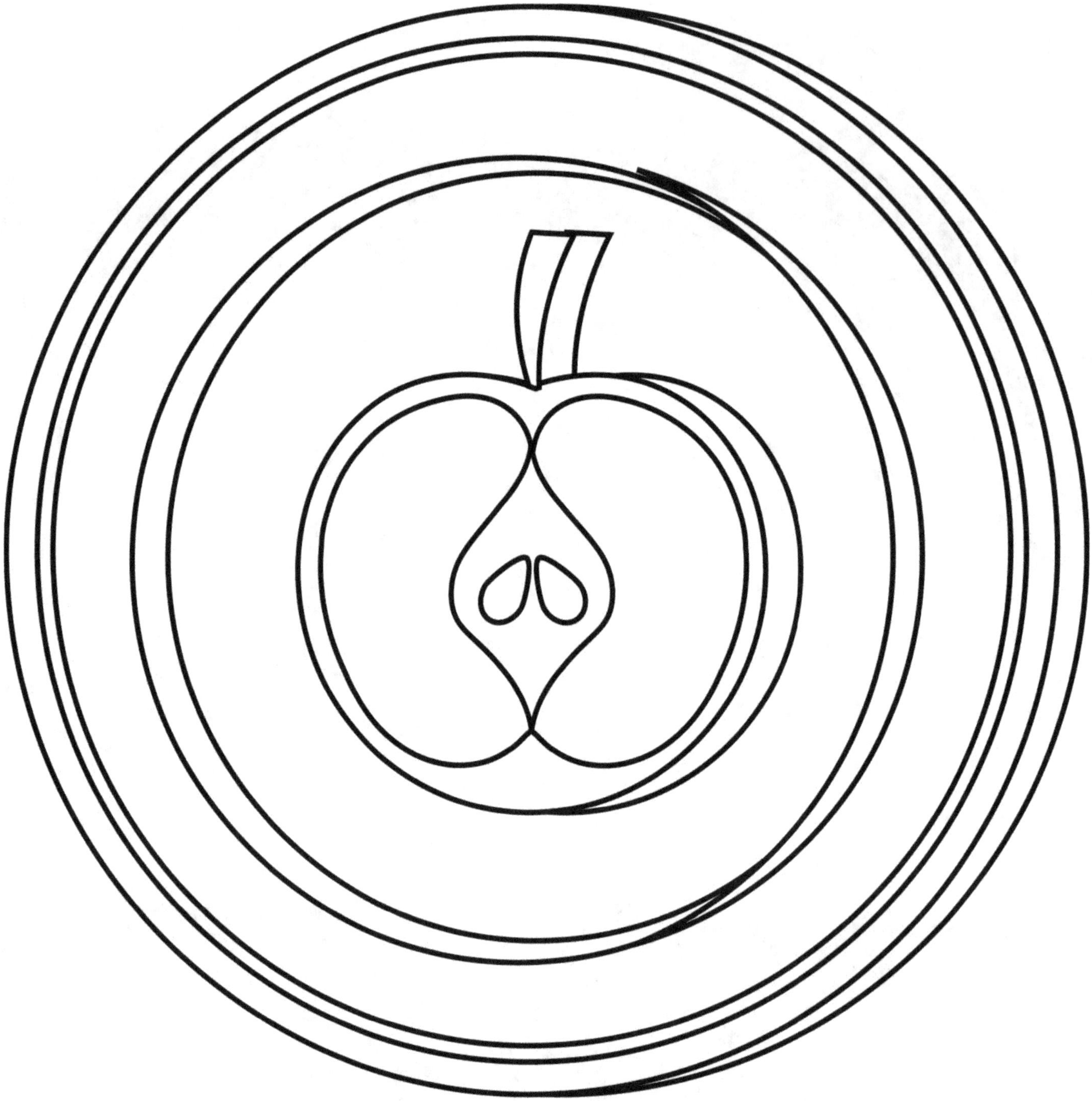

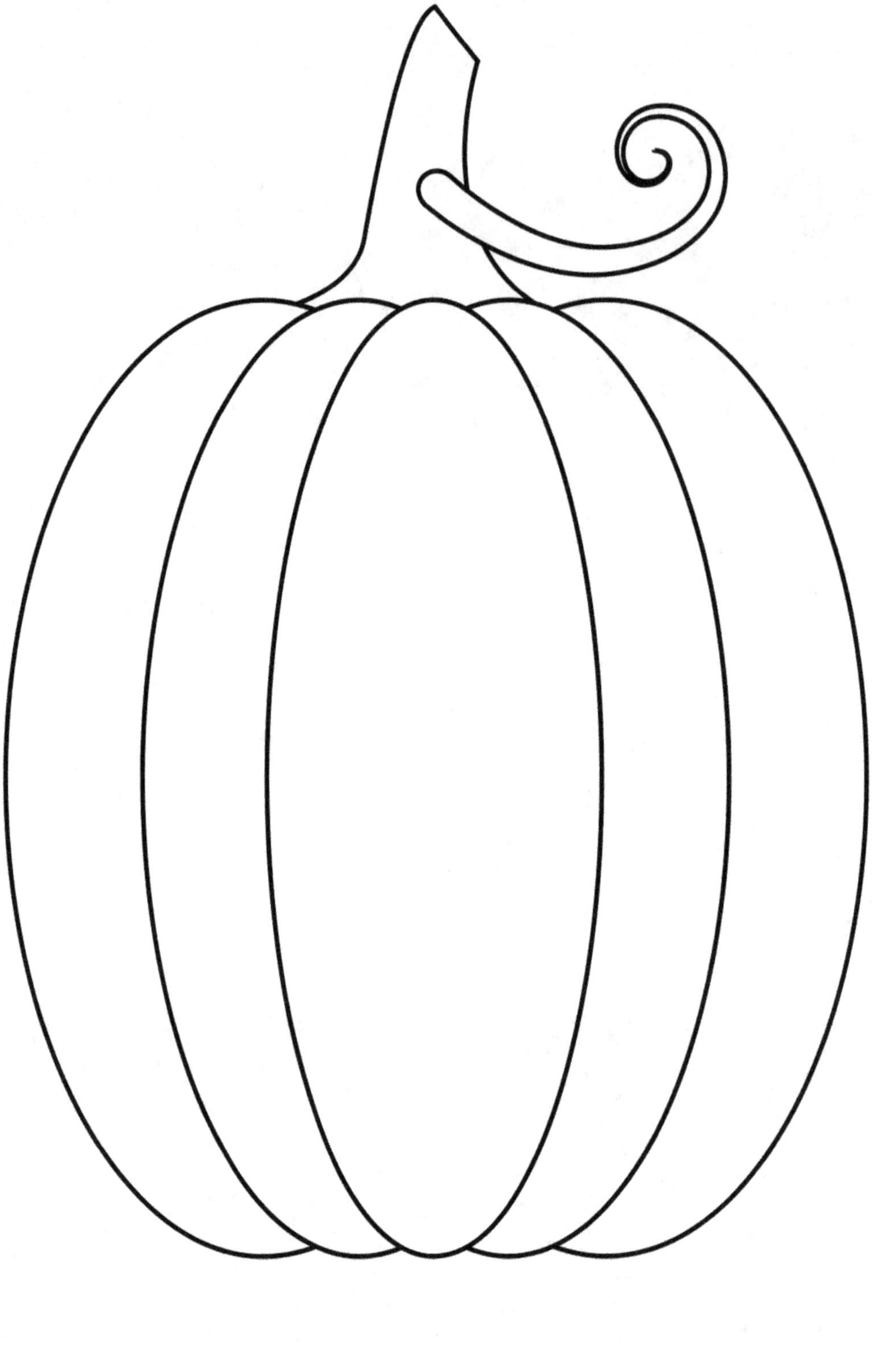

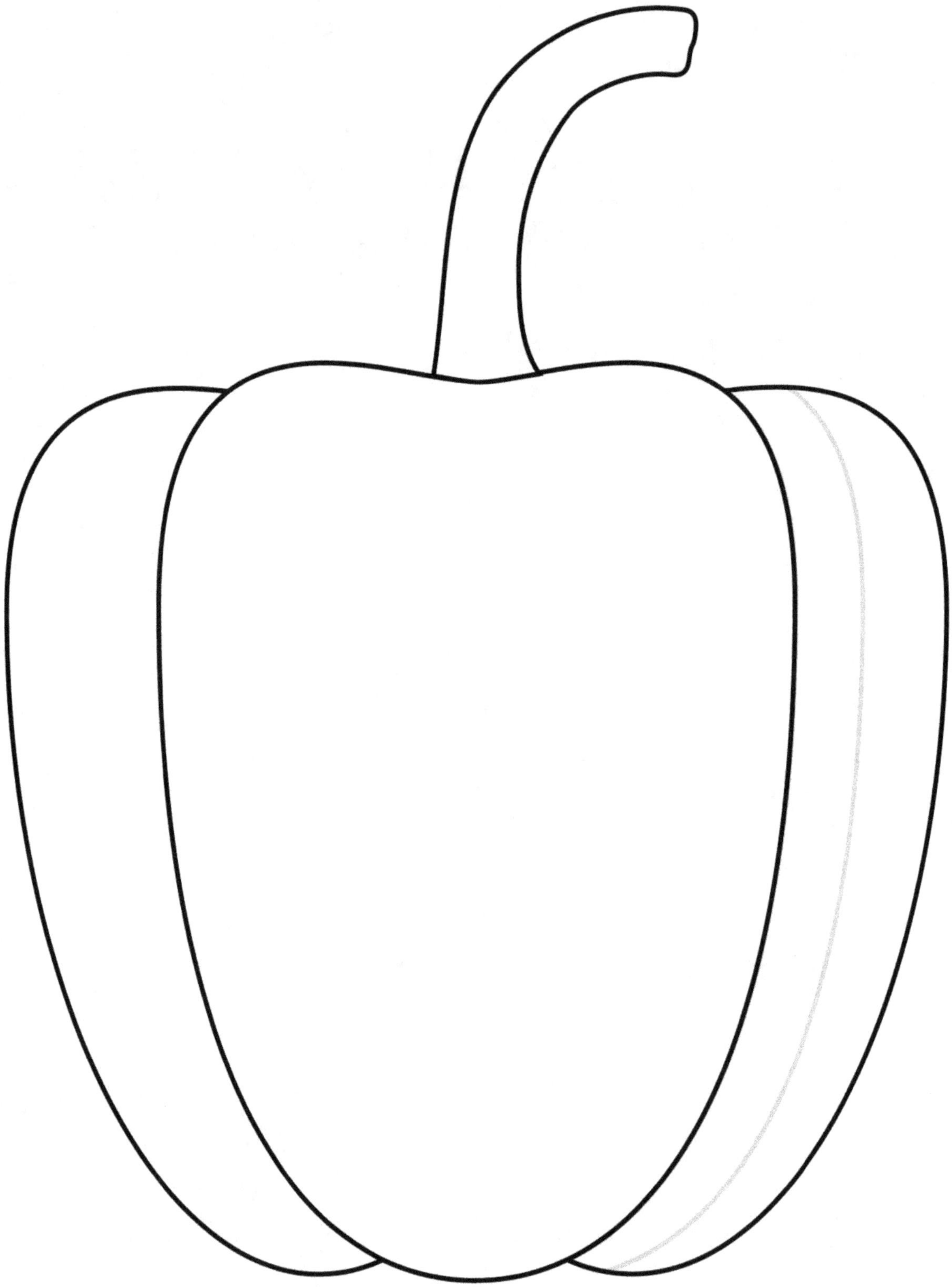

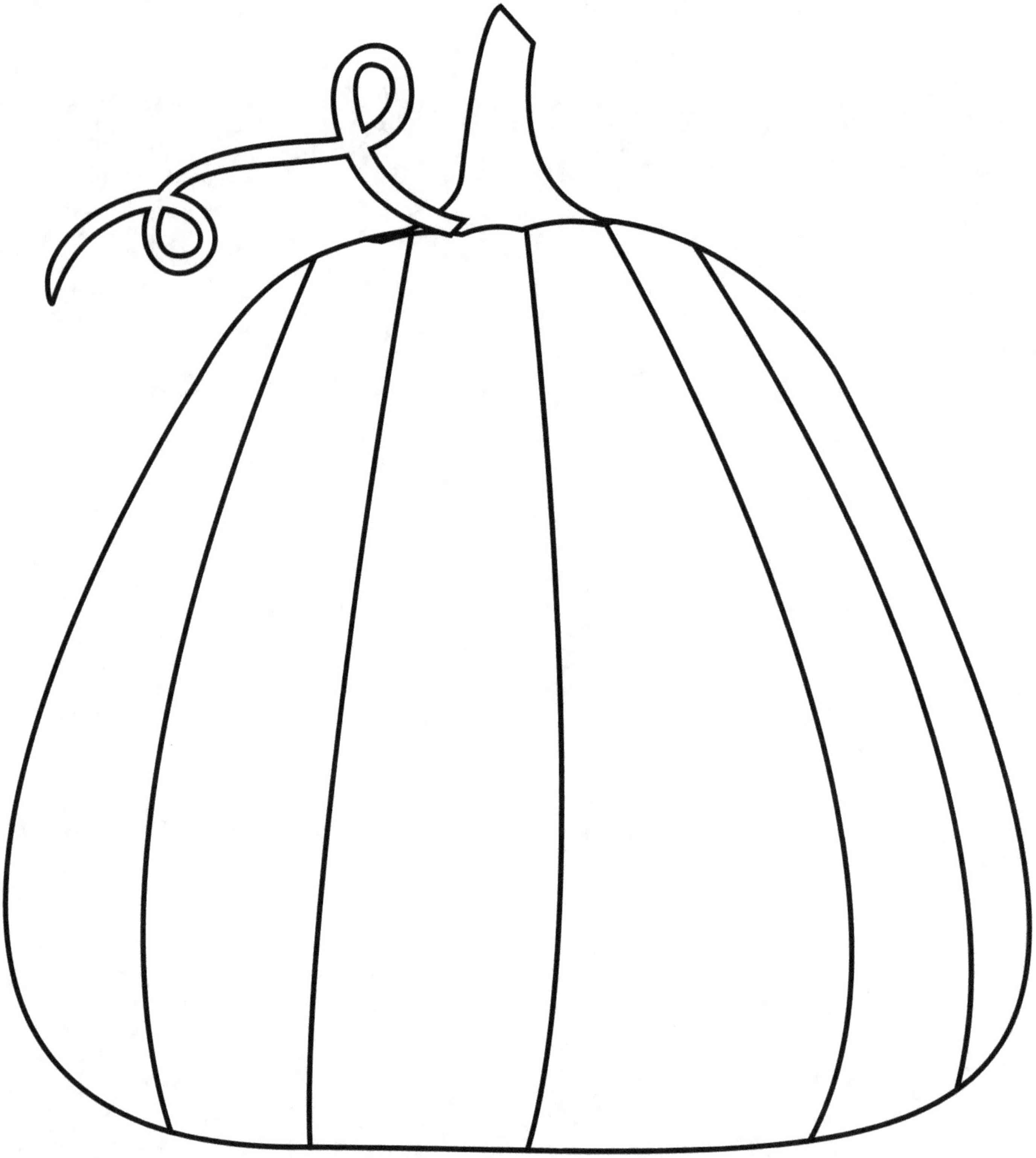

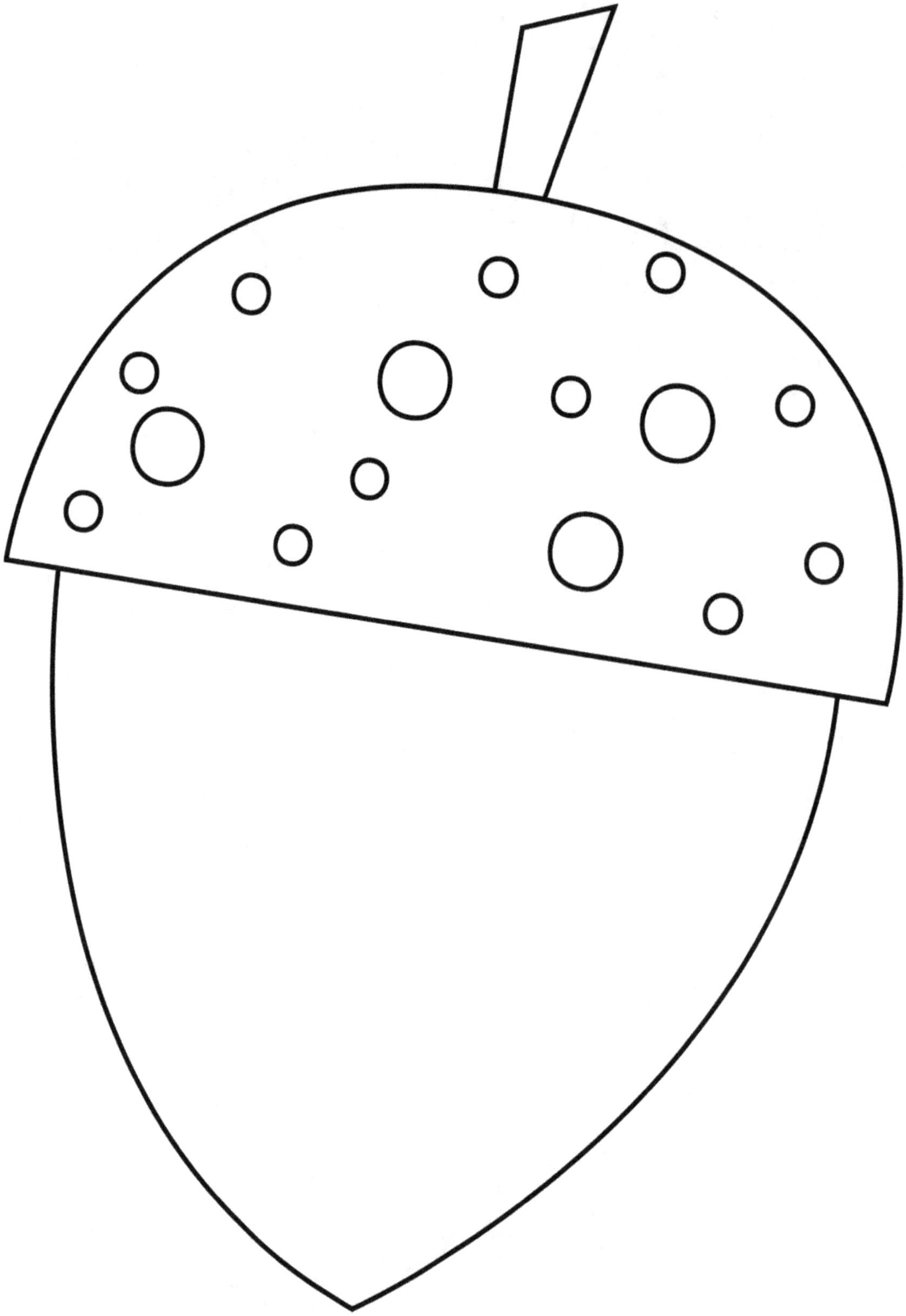

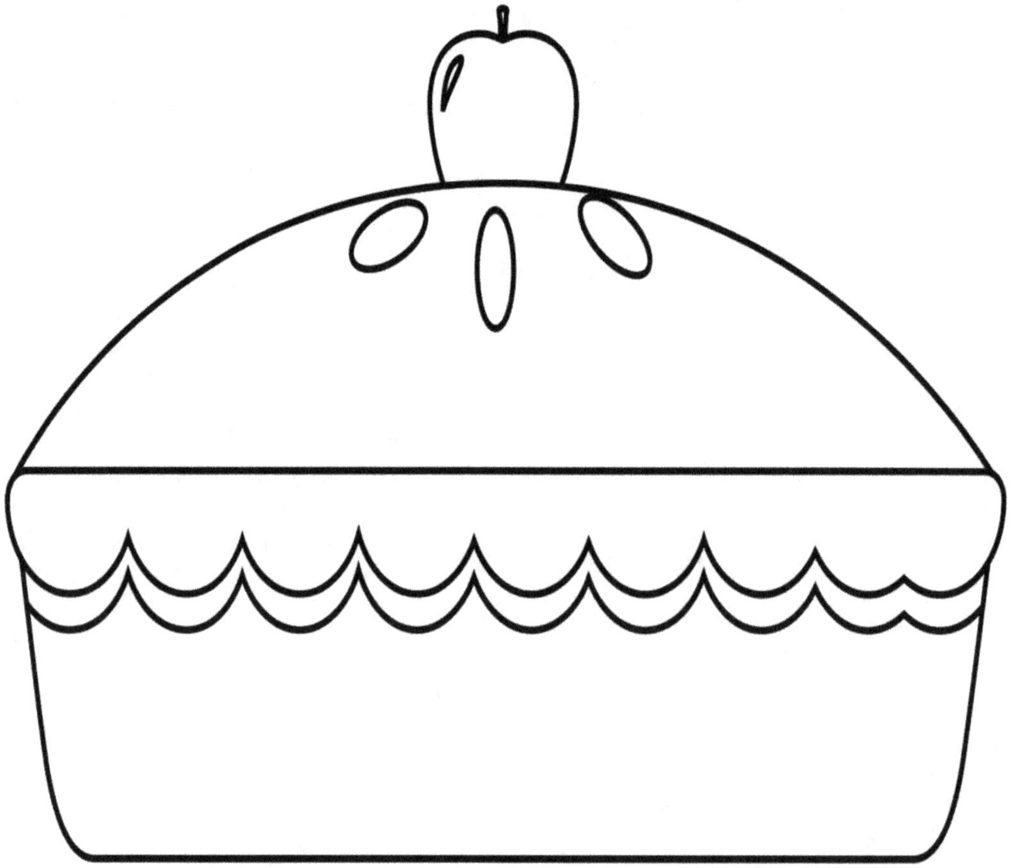

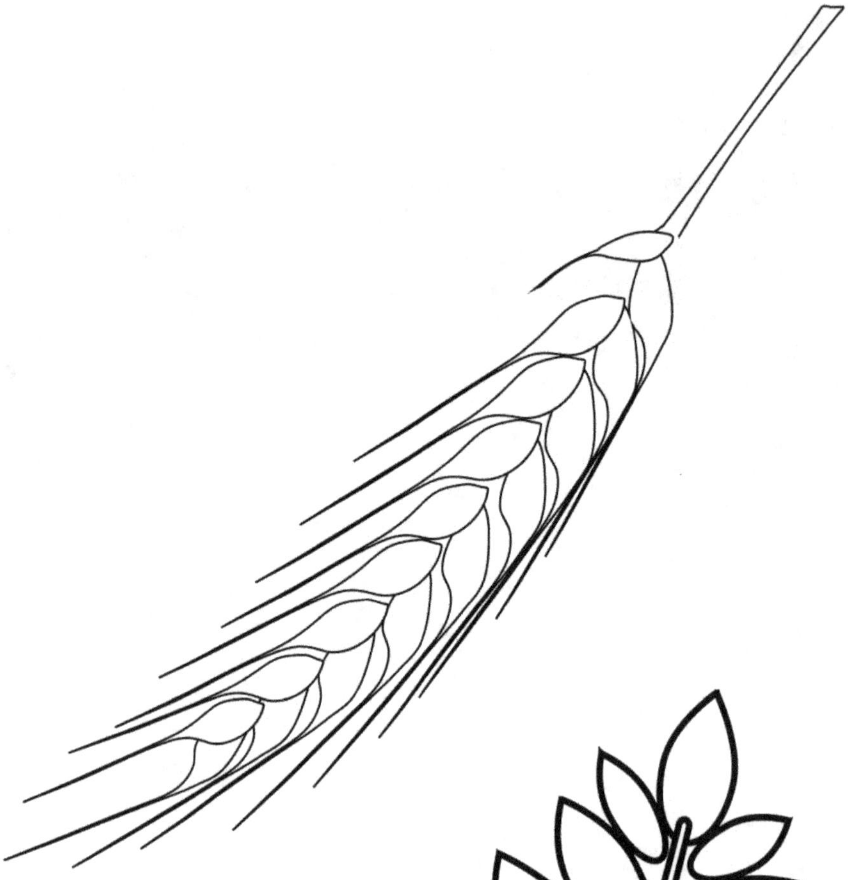
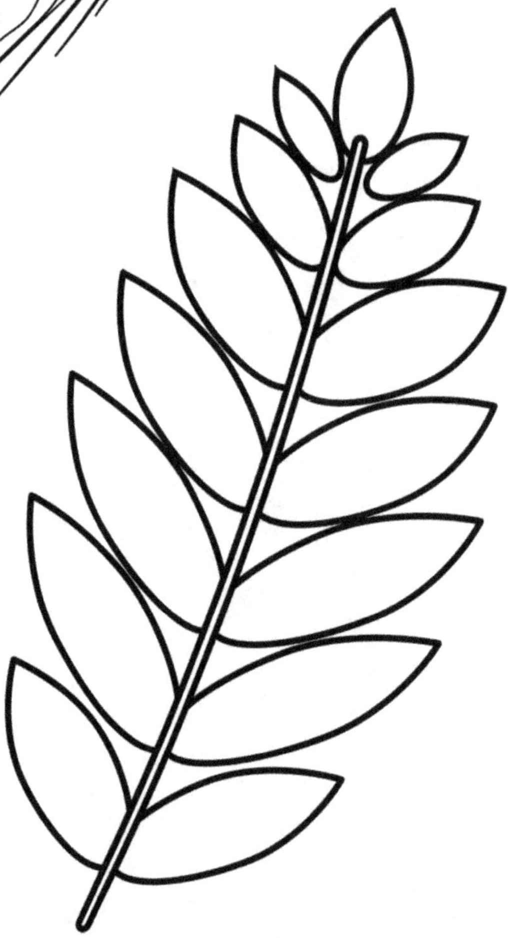

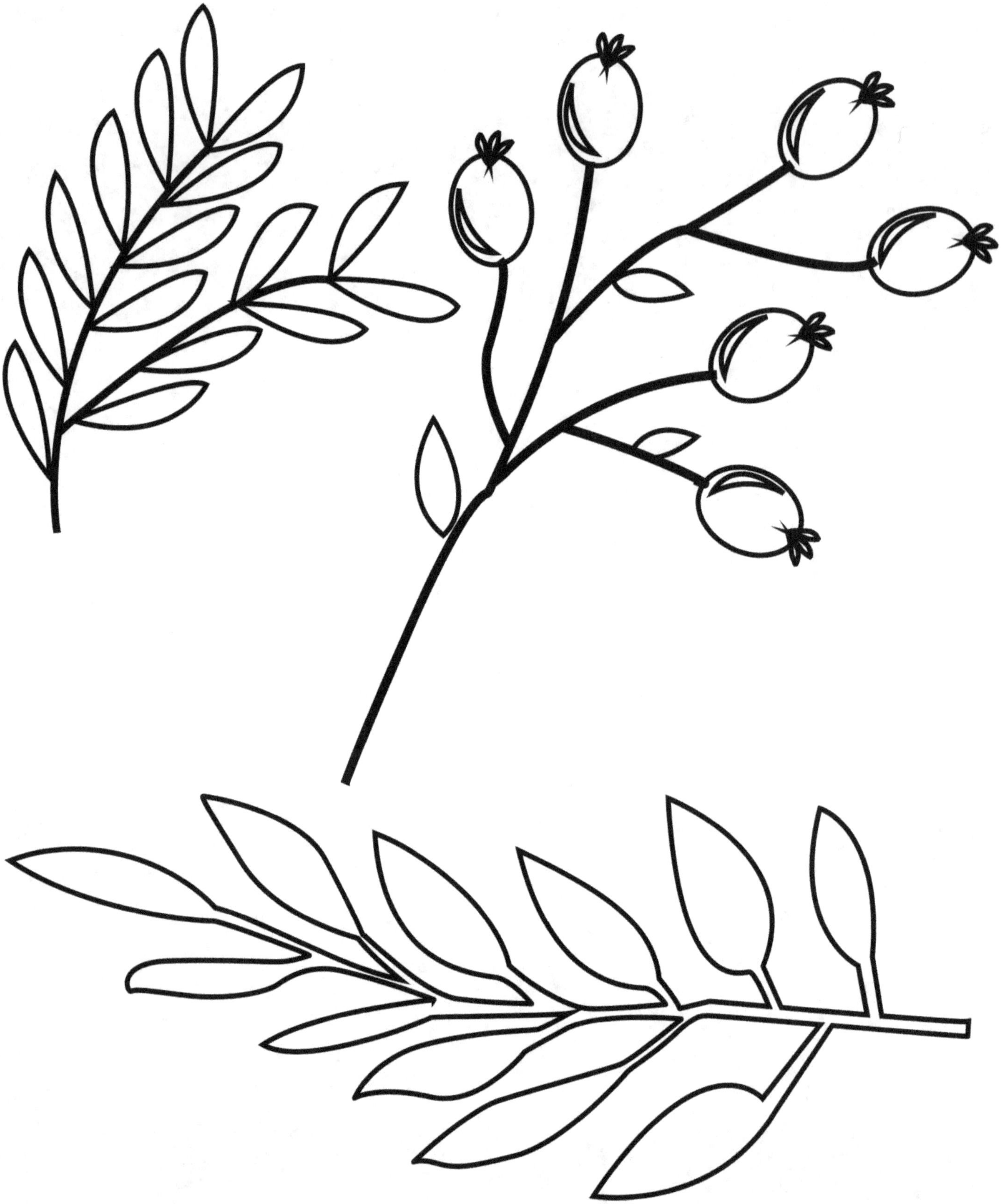

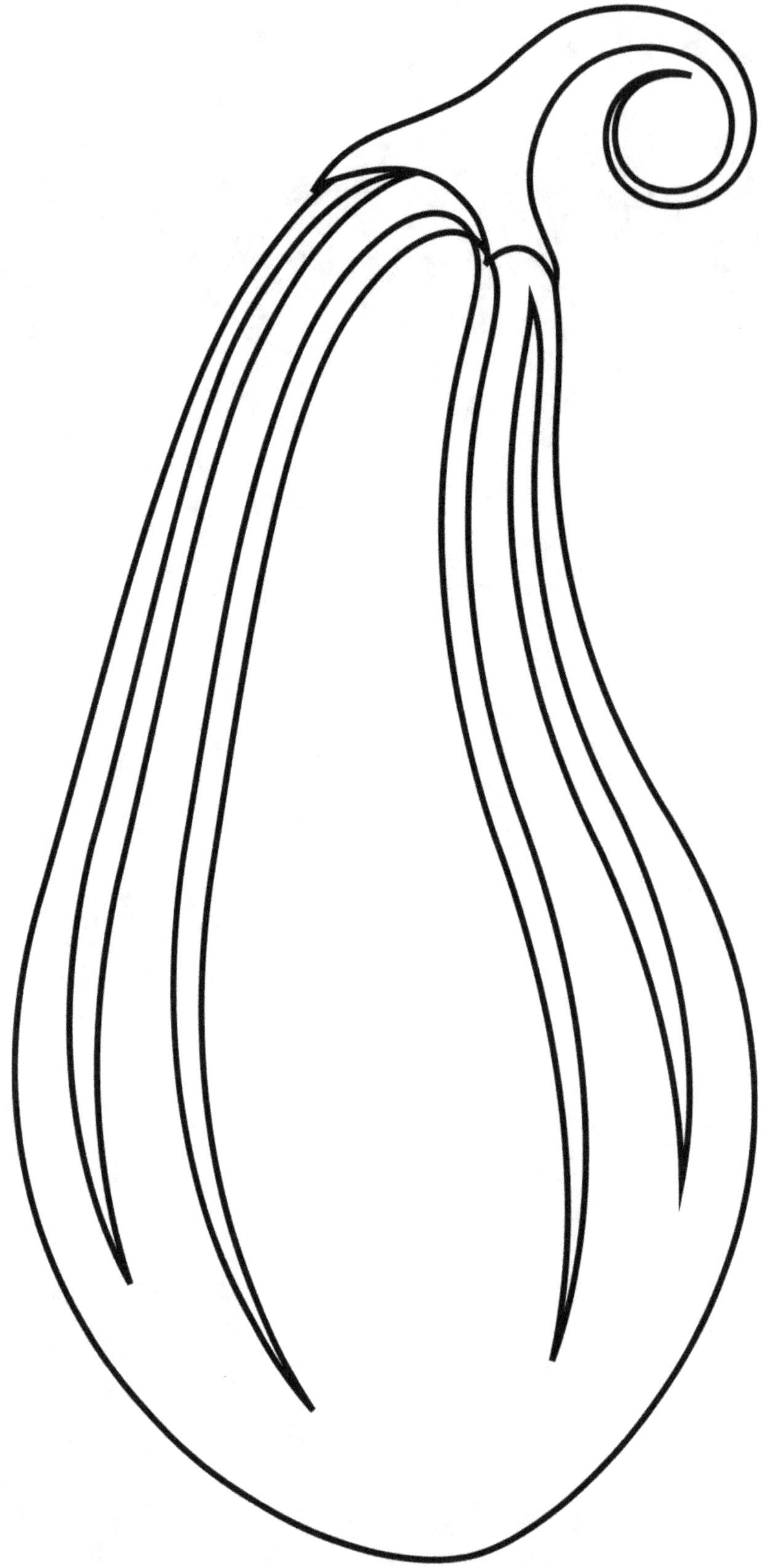

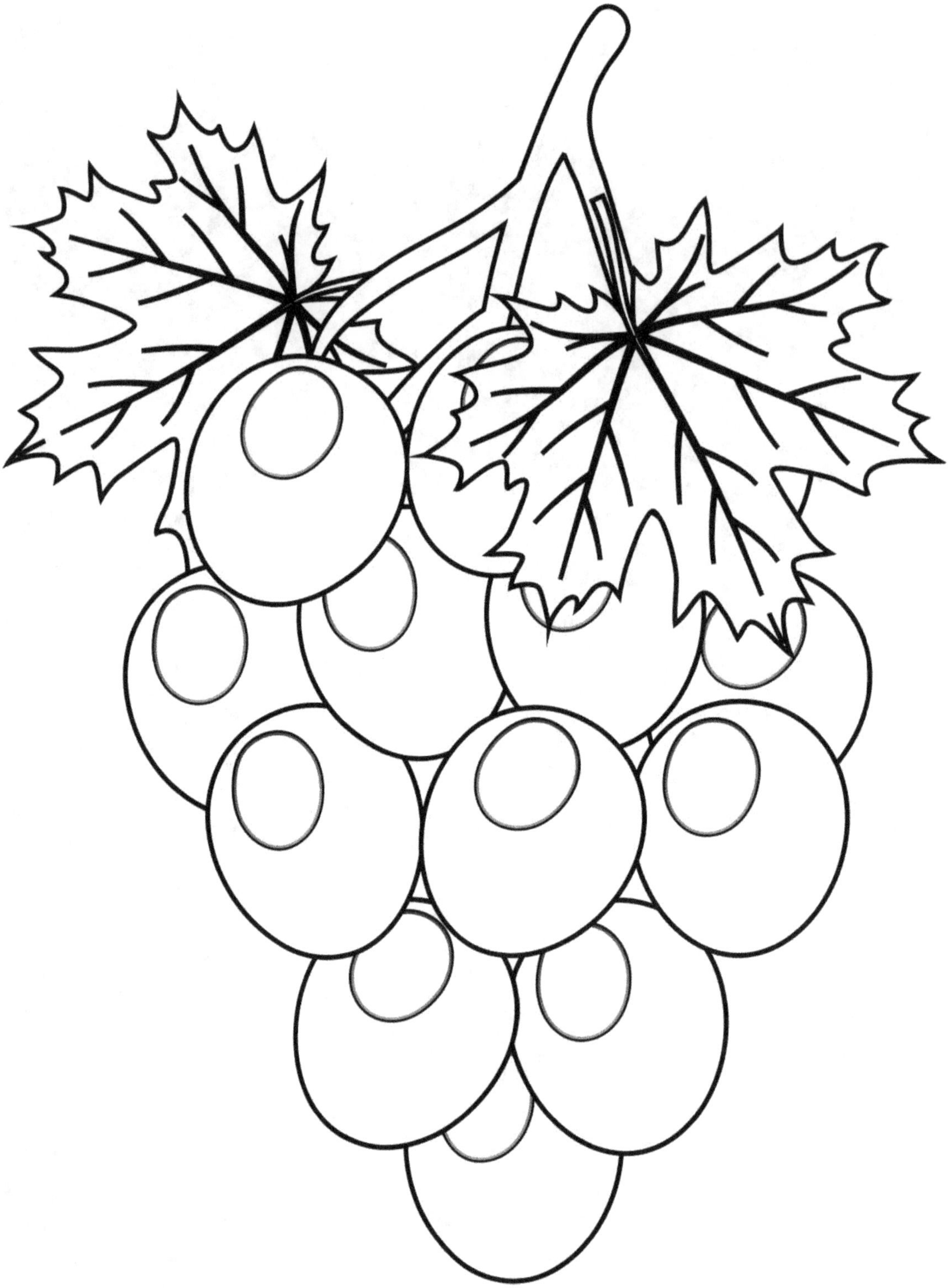

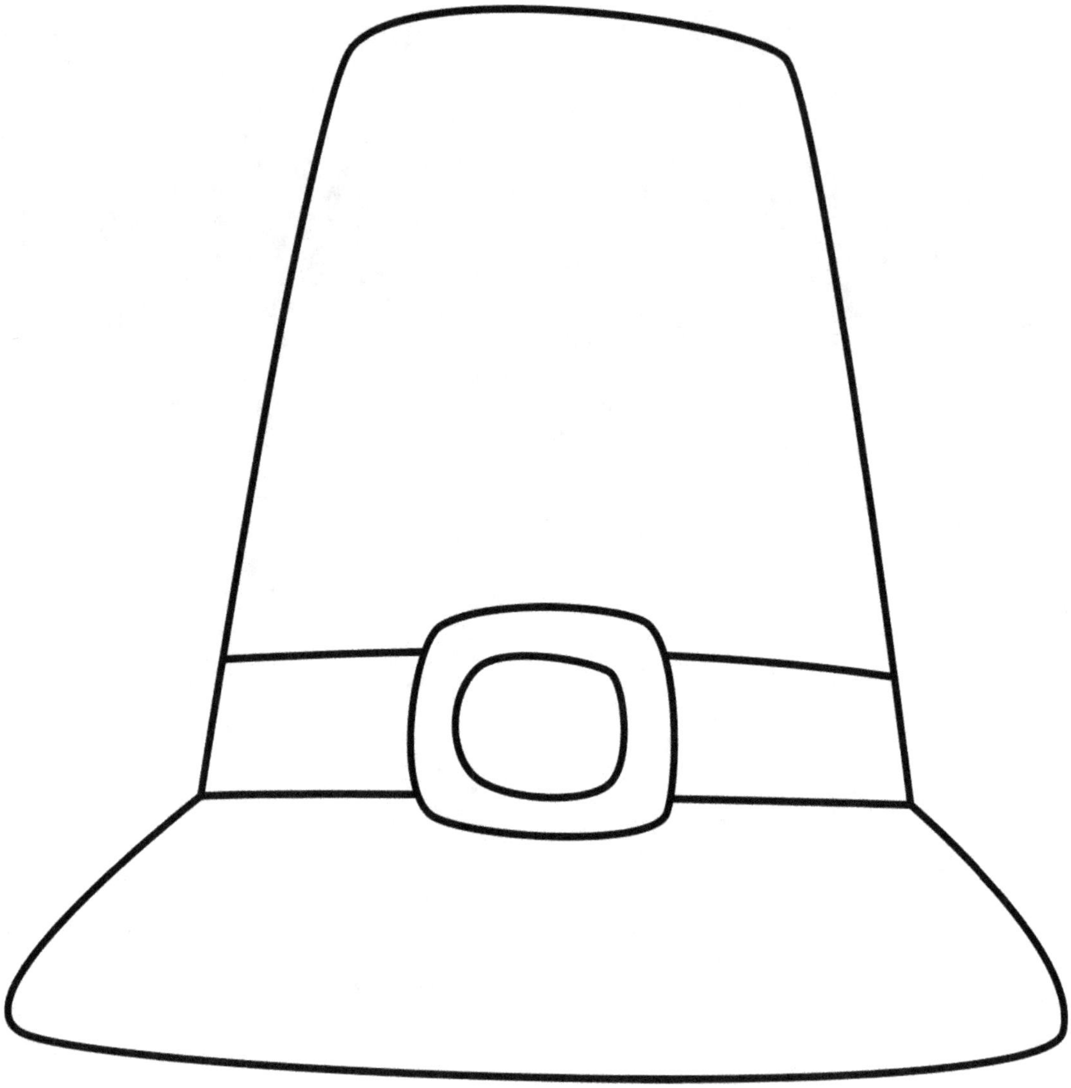

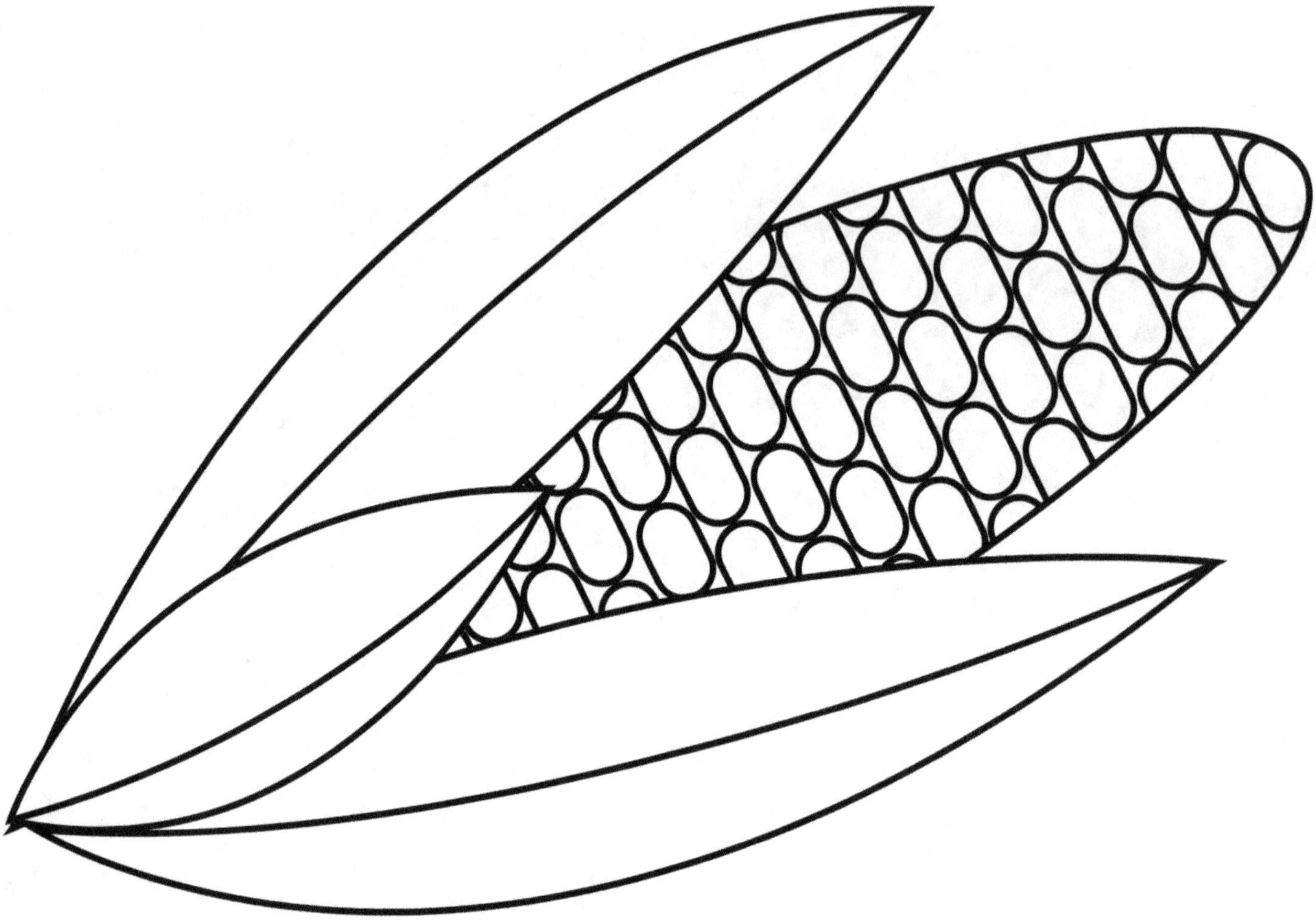

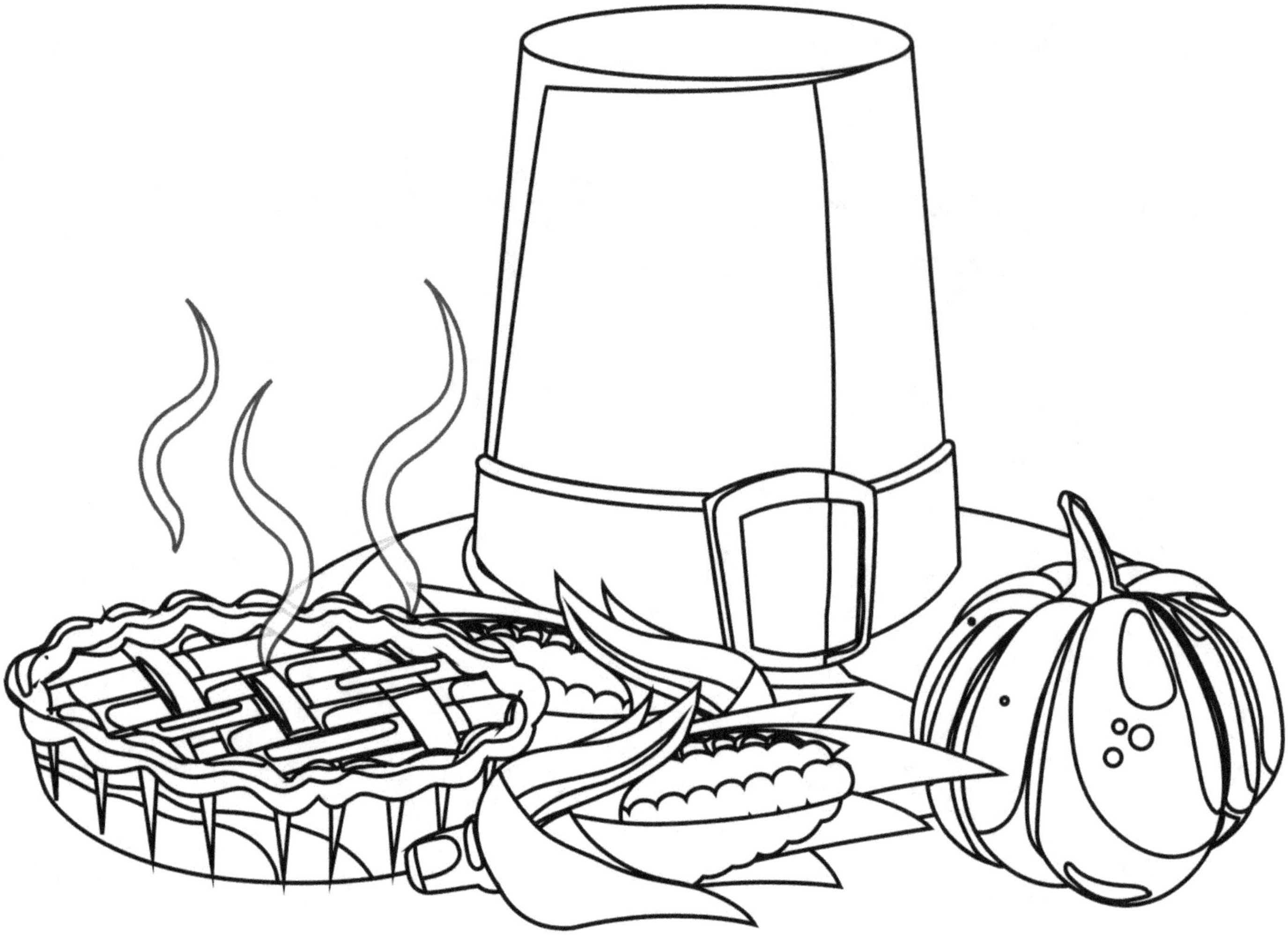

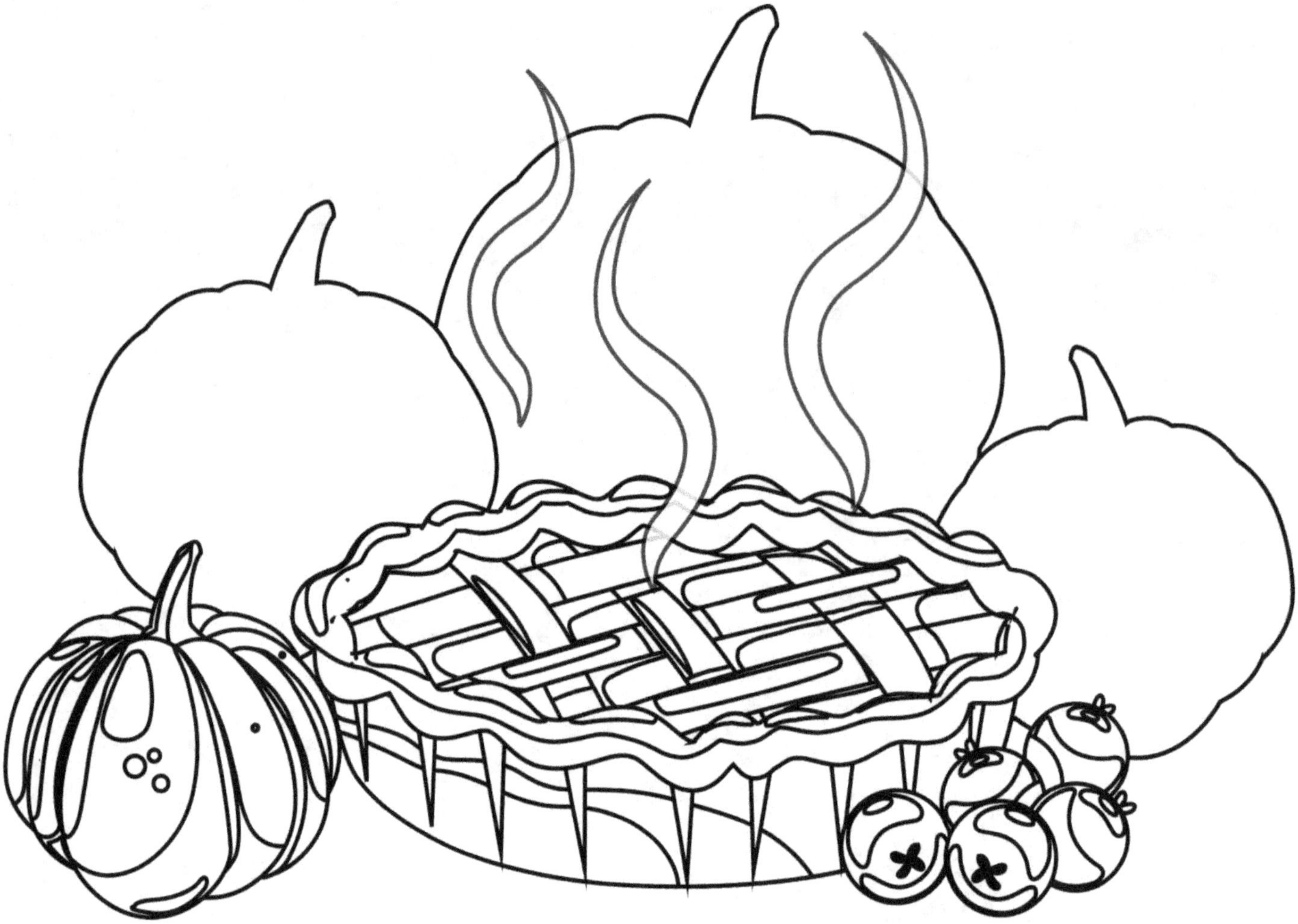

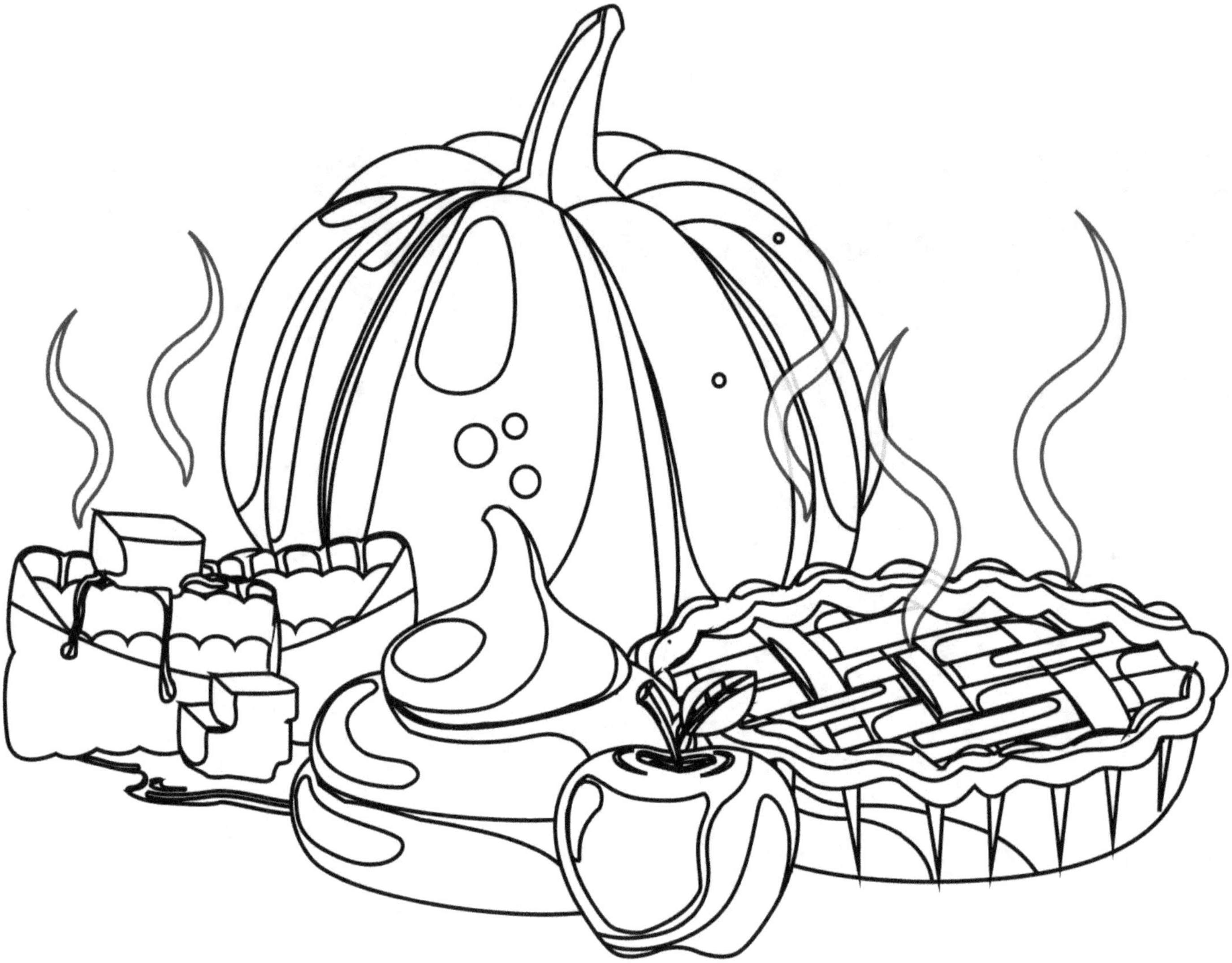

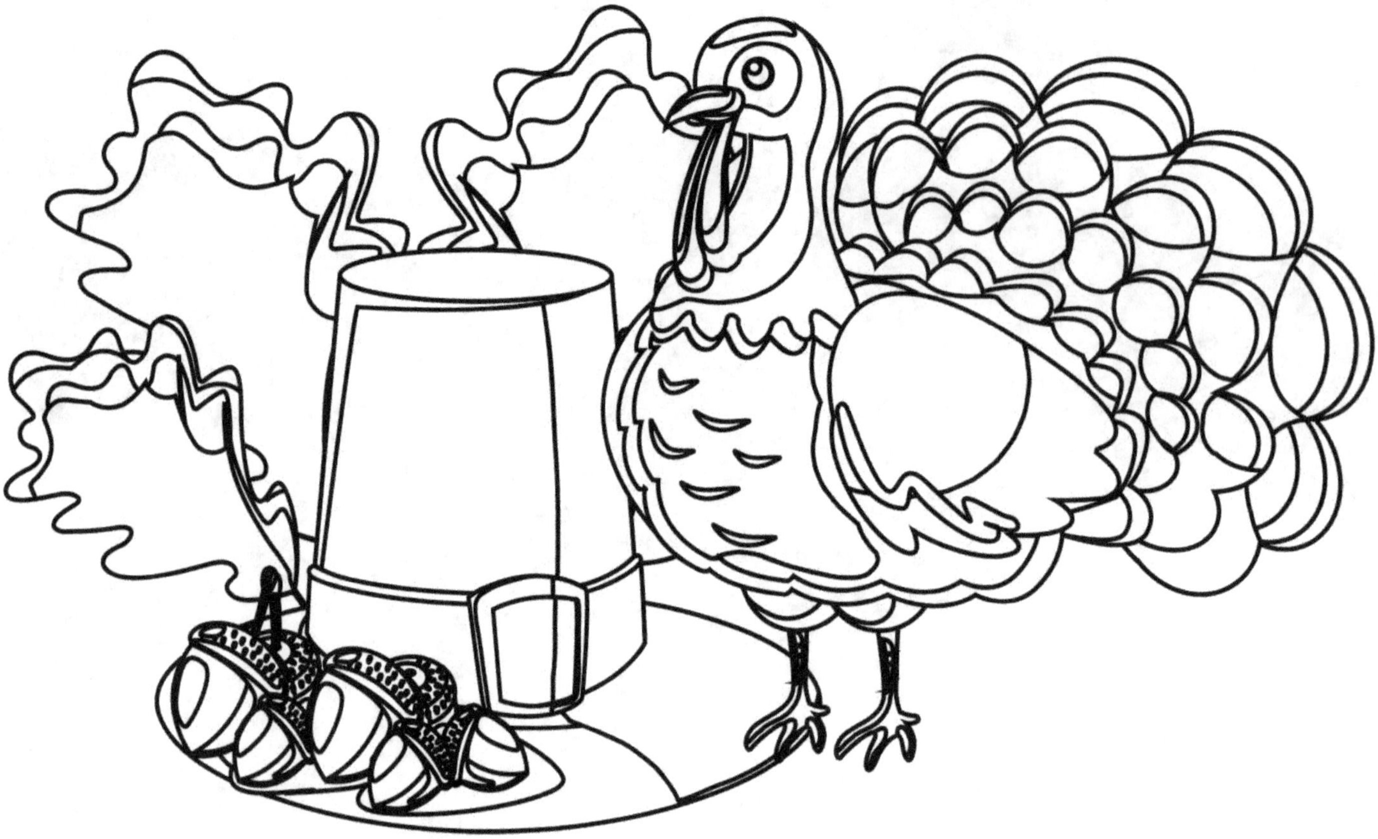

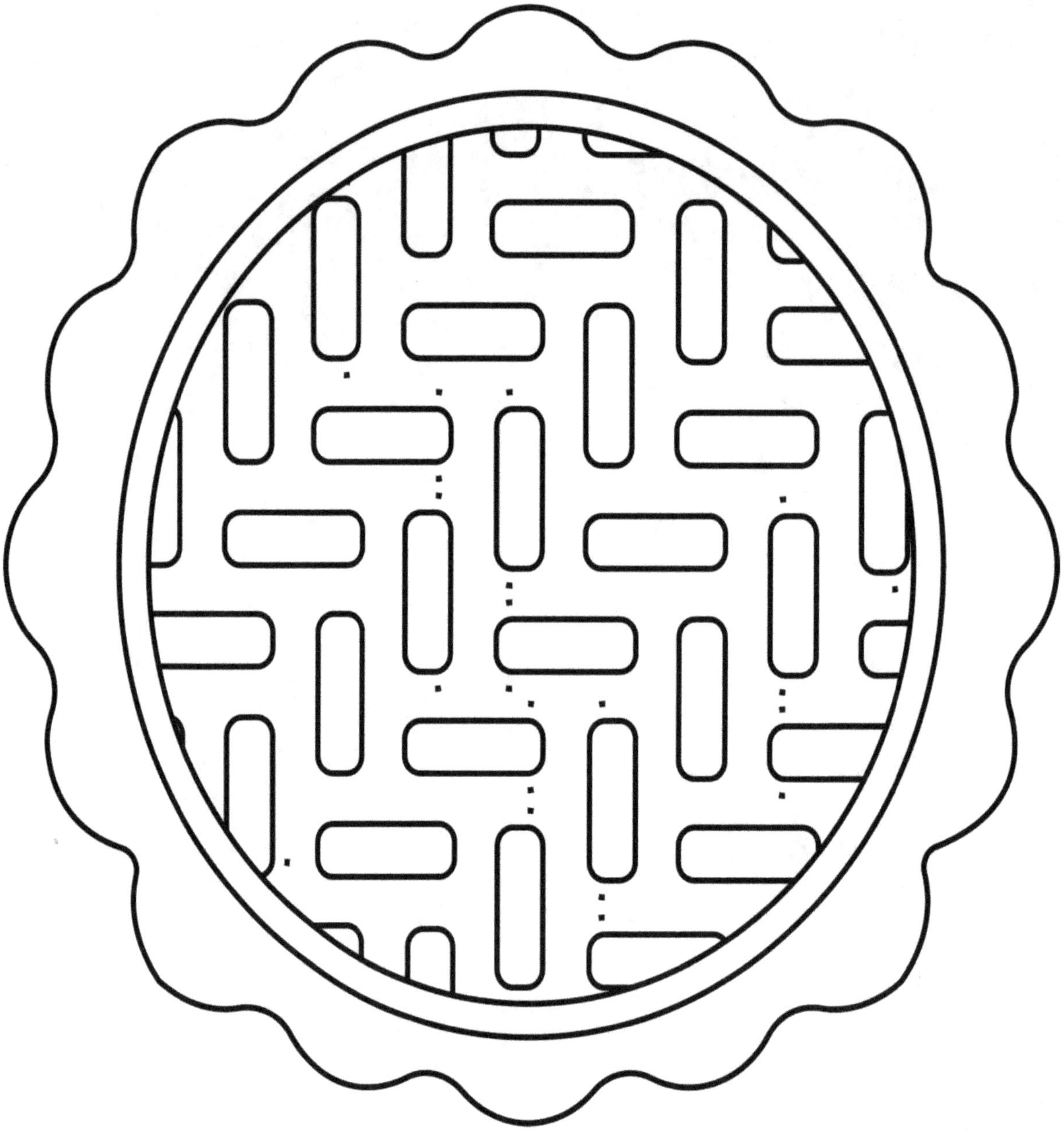

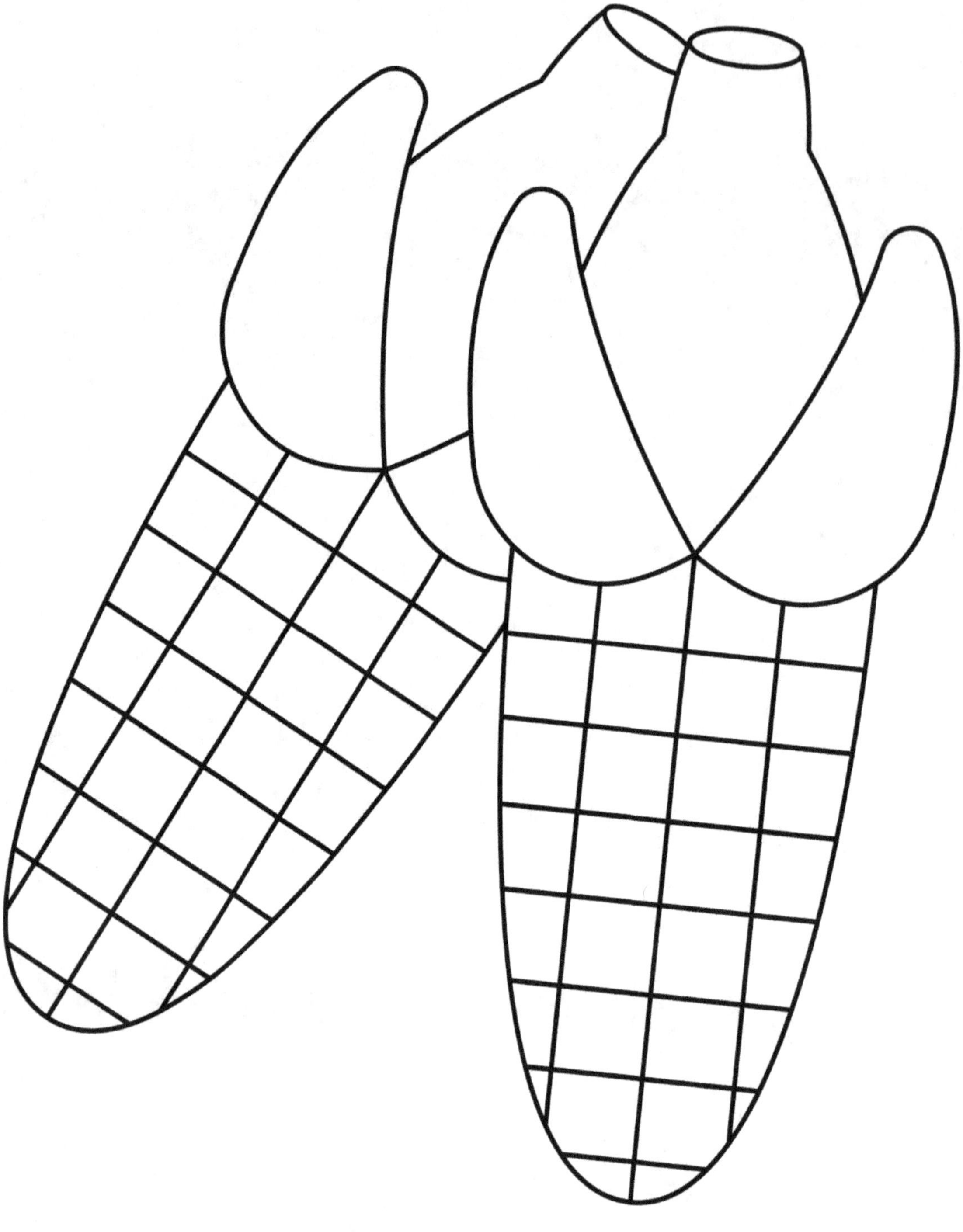

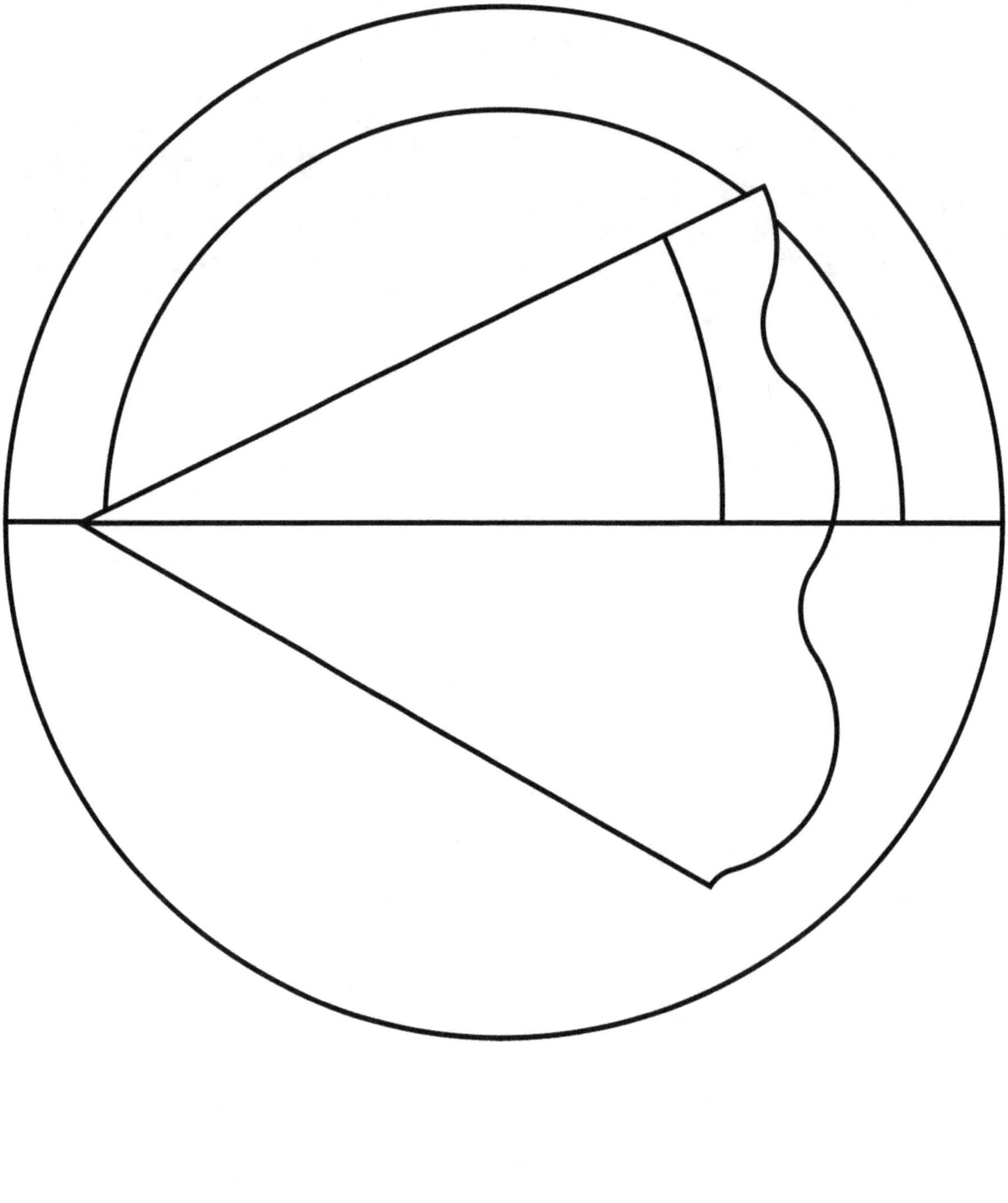

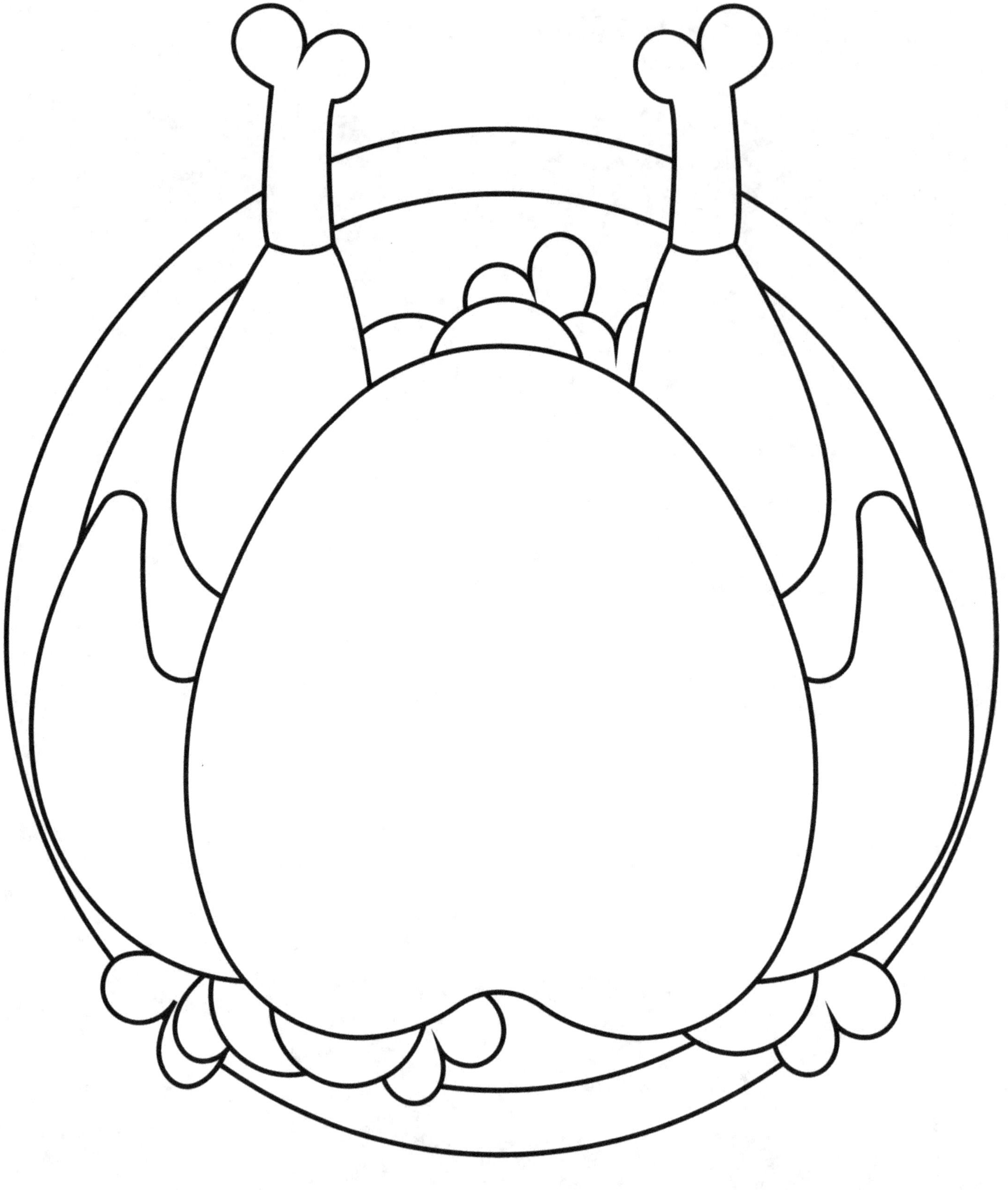

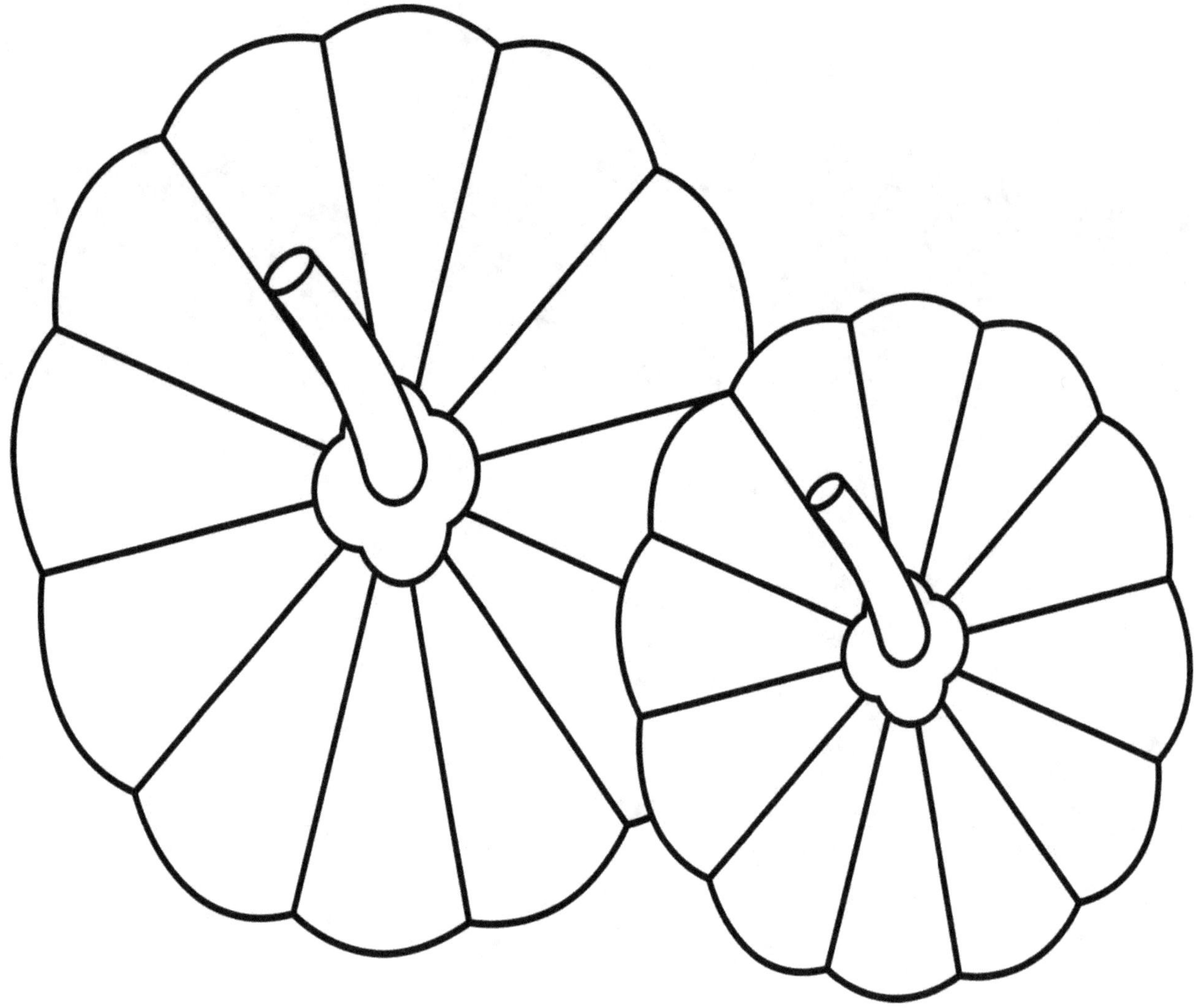

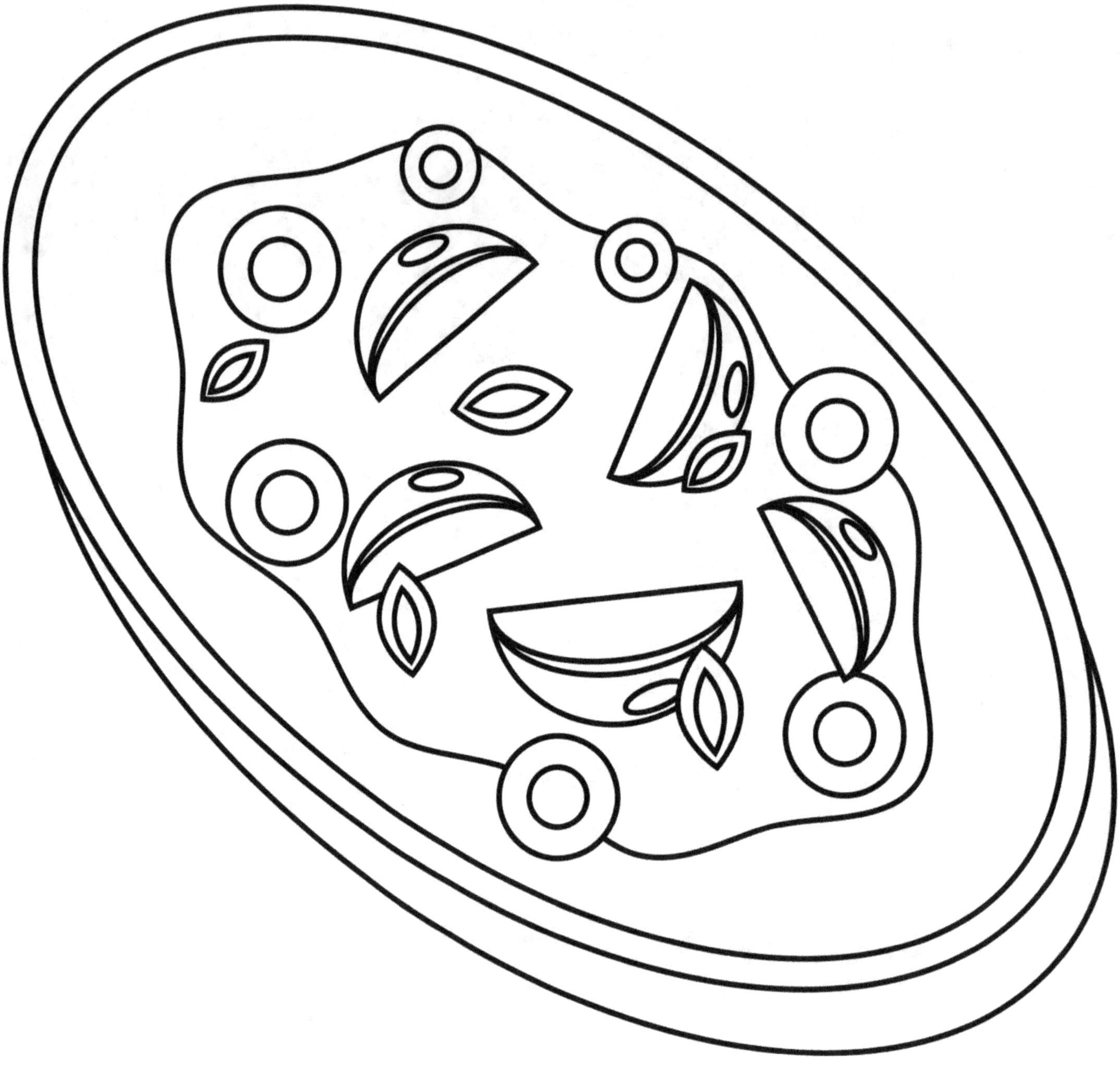

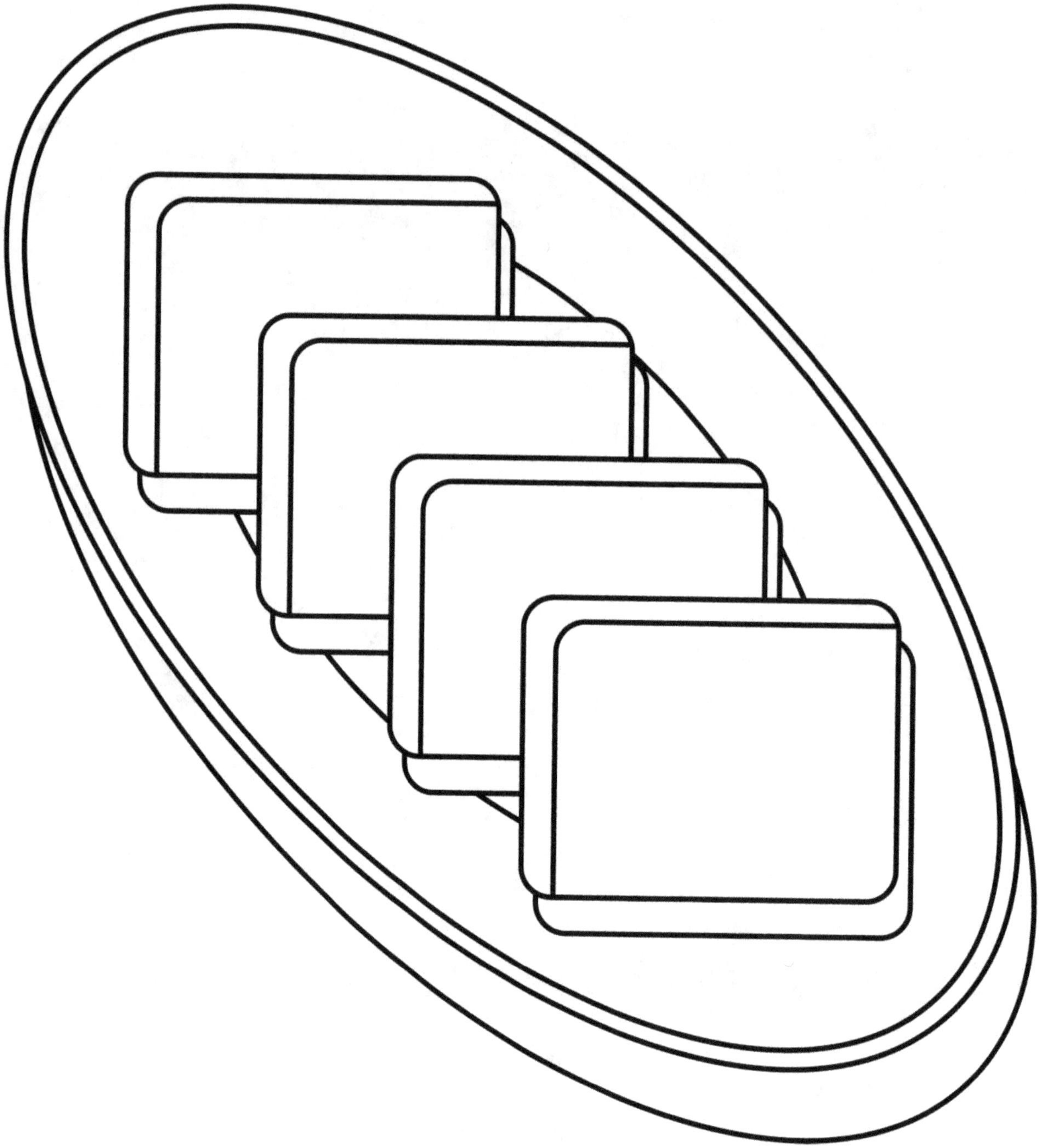

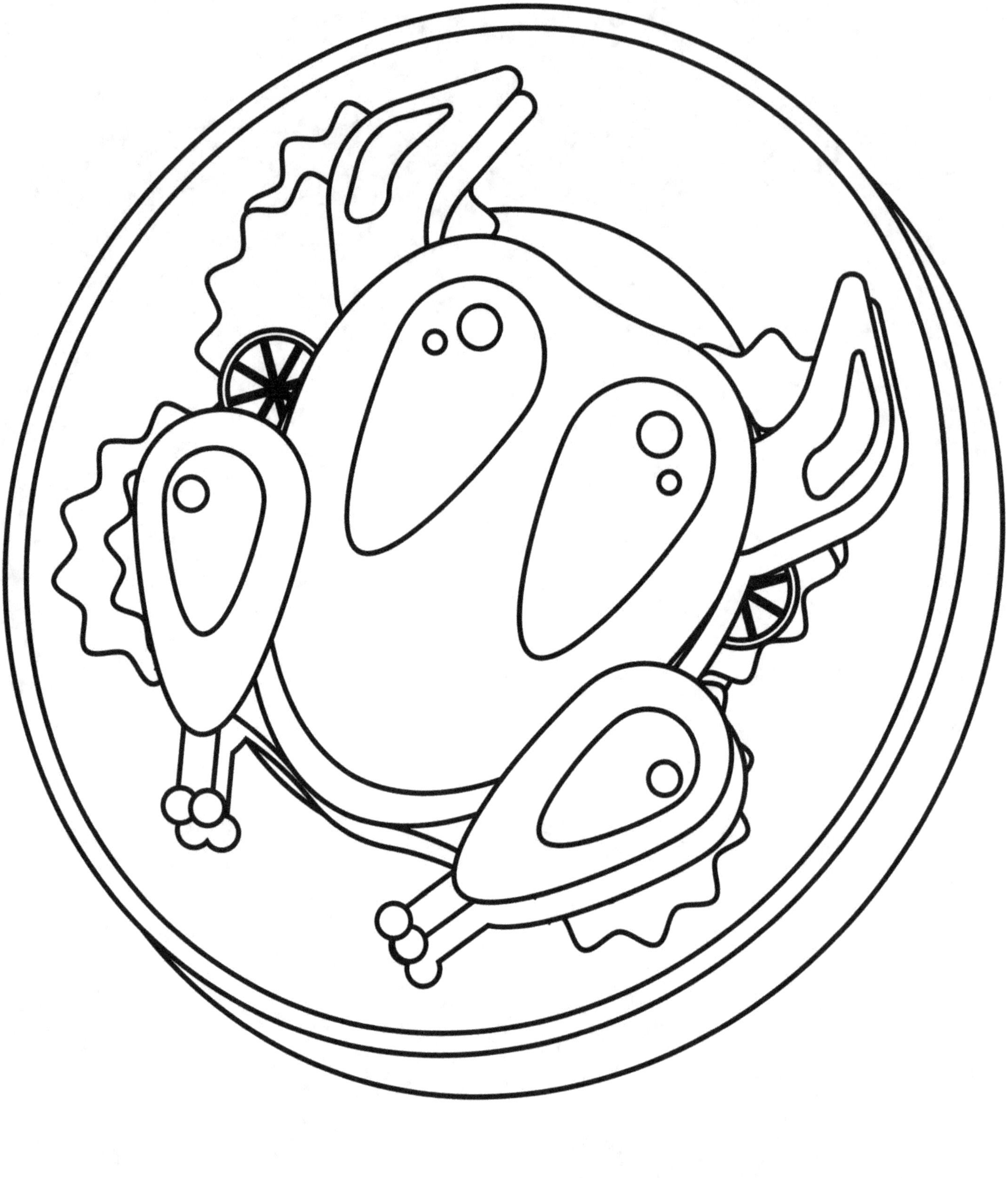

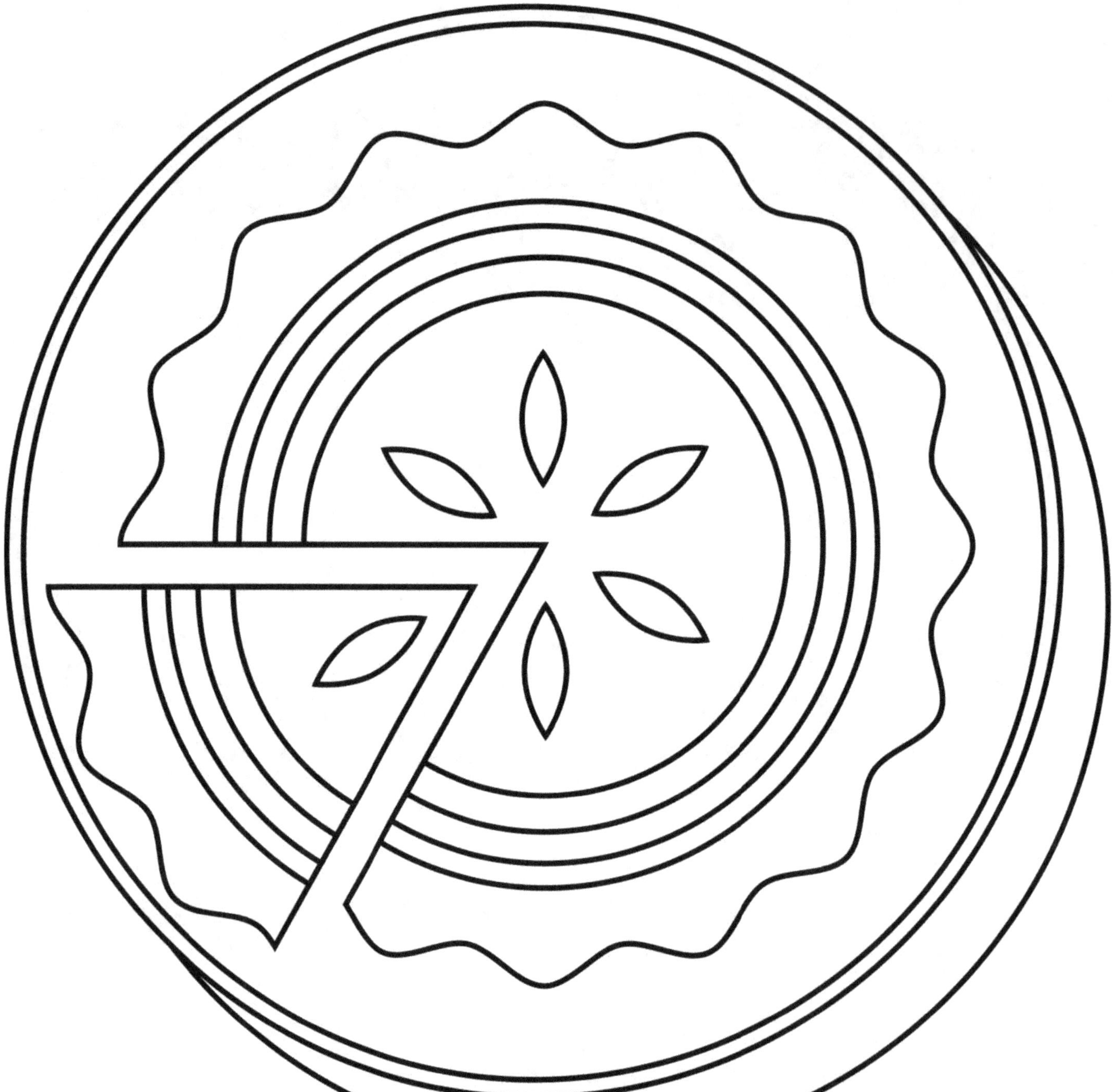

www.ingramcontent.com/pod-product-compliance
Lightning Source LLC
Chambersburg PA
CBHW080604220526
45466CB00010B/3246
* 9 7 9 8 5 5 2 6 4 8 7 0 2 *